Obituary

This book is dedicated to the memory of the author
Gordon D Findlay.
He passed away suddenly at the time this book
was being published.

".....to be absent from the body is to be present with the Lord"
2 Corinthians 5:8

1942 - 2005

My Hand on the Tiller

(a log of my life afloat)

Gordon D Findlay

authorHOUSE

1663 Liberty Drive, Suite 200
Bloomington, Indiana 47403
(800) 839-8640
www.AuthorHouse.com

© 2006 Gordon D Findlay. All Rights Reserved.

No part of this book may be reproduced, stored in a retrieval system, or transmitted by any means without the written permission of the author.

First published by AuthorHouse 01/23/06

ISBN: 1-4208-5894-7 (sc)

Printed in the United States of America
Bloomington, Indiana

This book is printed on acid-free paper.

This book is dedicated to my late father Bill Findlay
who first put my hand on a tiller.

OUT ON THE SEA

Hate you duplicity,
Rush after wealth?
Love you simplicity,
Honesty, health?
Go where God's air is free,
Breathe in its purity,
Take you a boat, and be
Out on the sea

Seek you a holiday
Where worries cease?
Leave you the crowded way,
Long you for peace?
Find you some sparkling bay,
Where all the world's at play,
Make you a merry May
Out on the sea.

Harold Padwick

Table of Contents

Foreword	ix
Chapter 1 - Early Days	1
Chapter 2 - Learning to Sail	11
Chapter 3 - The German Connection	23
Chapter 4 - International 8 metres	31
Chapter 5 - "Doon the Watter"	47
Chapter 6 - "Tir nan og"	59
Chapter 7 - Classic Yachts	79
Chapter 8 - Tall Ships	105
Chapter 9 - Loose Ends	135
Chapter 10 - Epilogue	145
Appendix 1 - Details of yachts	149
Appendix 2 - Details of tall ships	157
Appendix 3 - Sailing Vessel Rigs	161
Appendix 4 - Clyde Cruising Club Song	163
Appendix 5 - The Seaman's Language, a glossary	165
Appendix 6 – Useful Websites	177

Foreword

This is not an account of spectacular voyages or tales of survival at sea in storms and hurricanes but simply a collection of my experiences and memories as a yachtsman over half a century; a sort of log book of my life. I am not a professional writer but I have an urge to put some of my experiences on paper. I was blessed to be born into a sailing family and all my childhood holidays were spent aboard yachts, mainly cruising on the West Coast of Scotland. I have also had opportunities to sail on a number of famous yachts and sailing ships over the years. I hope this book will be of interest to yachtsmen who know this part of the world or who are interested in the details of the wide variety of yachts and other sailing vessels described. I have always had an interest in sailing boats and ships of all types and I have taken advantage of every opportunity to sail on as many as possible. I have owned a variety of different boats and I make no apology for describing some of them in detail, as I believe that if you are like me, you will be interested in such things.

Note: The tonnage is referred to in the case of yachts is Thames Measurement which is a method of measuring the general size of the vessel. It was commonly used to describe the size of a yacht until the 1980's but is not used much today. The tonnage referred to in the chapter on Tall Ships is Gross Registered Tonnage which is the normal international standard measurement of merchant ships. The formula for Thames Measurement is shown below.

$$\frac{(L - B) \times B \times \tfrac{1}{2}B}{94}$$ L = length between perpendiculars: B = Extreme Beam

Measurements of all vessels are in feet. L.O.A. is the abbreviation for overall hull length excluding bowsprits or other overhanging spars or fittings.

(Metric conversion 1 Foot = 0.3048 Metres)

Chapter 1 - Early Days

Although my father Bill Findlay was a yachtsman for most of his life, he only started sailing after he married my mother in 1935. He and his brother Donald were golfers, having played golf from childhood under the eye of my grandfather Andrew. Life members of Glasgow Golf Club at Killermont and Gailes where grandfather was captain, they spent every holiday and weekend on golf courses. With a handicap of 3 at his peak and a Scottish Boys Championship medal it was a surprise to his friends and family when Bill decided to buy a boat. As he was the type of person who always did things properly, he became so involved in sailing that he eventually gave up golf completely.

I believe this interest started during a holiday on the Norfolk Broads not long after his marriage to my mother Edna. I do know that shortly after this he bought a motor boat. He never talked much about it and soon exchanged it for his first sailing yacht. This was a 9 ton gaff sloop named *Llygra* (Argyll spelt backwards) designed and built by Robertsons of Sandbank in 1898. *Llygra* needed more crew than Bill, Edna and their spaniel dog Roy, so a mutual friend, Jimmy Black introduced them to a merchant navy officer, Harold Brown to join them on a west coast cruise during his leave. This led to Harold becoming a lifelong friend of the family and an excellent sailing companion. Although a professional seaman, Harold had sailed with Murray Blair as a young man in his yacht *Mimosa* and had some knowledge of small boats. Murray Blair was one of the founders of the Clyde Cruising Club. Jimmy Black had told Harold that his friends had a "big yacht", so not quite knowing what to expect, he brought along his white cotton trousers to be properly kitted out. Only on meeting Bill and Edna for the first time did he realise that size is relative and although Llygra was somewhat bigger than Jimmy Black's boat, she was certainly not a "big boat". The white trousers became Roy's bed in the forepeak!

Harold had a wonderful sense of humour and was an expert navigator. He taught navigation by profession at the Glasgow Technical College on coming ashore after the war - what a mentor for a new sailor! During the war Harold commanded a corvette on the North Atlantic convoys and although he always made light of it, this was a highly dangerous situation with enemy U boats sinking large numbers of Allied ships. Harold was awarded the D.S.C. with bar for sinking two U boats, ramming one with his ship and picking up the survivors. He recalled that these very young Germans came aboard terrified, expecting to be shot, only to be offered a cup of tea and dry clothing!

After the war my father sold *Llygra* and along with my Uncle Donald bought *Petula;* designed and built by the famous William Fife of Fairlie. *Petula* was a larger yacht of 18 tons. She was a gaff yawl of moderate displacement, indeed considered light by the standards of the day. Built at Fairlie in Scotland in 1899, she was fast and weatherly. This was the first boat I ever sailed in. An entry in *Petula's* log book of 1st June 1946 says I was aboard on a passage from Fairlie to Port Bannatyne. I have no recollection as I was only 3 years old but I always like to think how fortunate I was to start my sailing in a Fife yacht! The three generations of William Fifes were perhaps the most famous yacht designers of all time and yachts designed and built by Fife are still prized today for their timeless perfection and beauty.

Bill and Edna Findlay in Llygra

As time went on Bill and Donald decided to get a larger boat and sold *Petula* to "Blondie" Hasler who had become famous as one of the "Cockleshell Heroes" in World War II. He contributed much to sailing and organised the first single handed transatlantic race, participating in his "junk" rigged folkboat *Jester*. Hasler made several cruises during the years he owned *Petula*, perhaps the most noteworthy being his landing on Rockall, the tiny deserted rock out in the Atlantic west of Scotland. *Petula* was the first yacht ever to visit the rock.

Bill and Donald then bought the International Twelve Metre class yacht *Marina*, previously owned by Sir Henry Burton and raced successfully in the Solent pre-war Twelve Metre Class. Like so many others she had been laid up during the war and racing in Twelve Metres seemed to be over. Designed by Alfred Milne *Marina* was built at Bute Slip Dock in 1935. She was a beautiful yacht and the brothers' intention was to improve the accommodation to make her more suitable for family cruising, as by then I had a young brother Kenneth and a sister Joyce. Unfortunately as *Marina* was being towed to the Clyde by a tug she broke adrift in a gale and was wrecked on the Smalls rocks on the Welsh coast. What a sad end for such a fine vessel. Nothing daunted my father immediately bought another yacht. This was *Eileen*, another Fife. *Eileen* was one of two yachts to bear this name, both built for the Fulton family of Greenock by William Fife. Known as the *Wee Eileen* as she was the smaller of the two and anything but wee! Her overall length was 60 feet, built in 1935 and rigged as a bermudan cutter although originally designed as a yawl. Bill recalled that when he bought her at Fairlie Yacht Slip, Archie McMillan who had taken over the yard after William Fife died was unwilling to let him have the mizzen mast which my father rightly expected to belong to the boat. He was asked to pay extra for it, so *Eileen* remained a cutter. In more recent times *Eileen* had been re-named *Aquarius*, based in the Pacific but she has been brought back to Europe and at the time of writing she is awaiting restoration to her original condition in Belgium.

My father mainly raced in *Eileen* with his all male crew. These were all experienced yachtsmen – Bill Findlay, Harold Brown, Jimmy Matheson, Colin McPhail, Jimmy Robin, Jimmy Webster, Alistair McDonald and Barry Summers were the regulars and wives and children sometimes came along for cruising weekends. Each year we rented a house at Hunter's Quay for July and August where *Eileen* was moored at the Royal Clyde Yacht Club. My father travelled by steamer to Gourock and train to business in Glasgow. It seemed so much easier in these days! At that time a large fleet of yachts moored at Hunter's Quay. The club had a beautiful white launch with Mr. Waddell the club boatman ferrying crews aboard and ashore from their yachts. My interest at that time was in Clyde steamers and I remember the *Jeannie Deans, Caledonia, Lucy Ashton, the Duchesses of Hamilton and Montrose* amongst others.

One memory of a day in *Eileen* when I was about 6 years old was when our uncle, aunt and cousins from South Africa were aboard for a sail to the Gareloch. The adults were having an enjoyable midday glass (or two) of champagne to celebrate the visit and my grandfather was at the helm. As he had absolutely no idea about sailing and as my father was a little distracted, he took *Eileen* the wrong side of the buoy at Rhu narrows. The channel was much narrower at that time and it was the top of high water! Needless to say *Eileen* went aground on Rhu spit and we children were taken ashore to the Queen's Hotel in Helensburgh for the night. To the *Eileen* crew's acute embarrassment, members of the Royal Northern Yacht Club walked round her after dinner as she lay undamaged on her side high and dry.

Jimmy Robin, one of the *Eileen* crew kept amusing logs of those days. One entry describes how Alistair McDonald who was disabled and tended to stay below in bad weather, poked his head out the main hatch on day on a stiff windward beat to say "the barometer has fallen" He was met with the caustic reply "of course it has you idiot" He tried to explain that the barograph had fallen off its shelf onto his head! Jimmy also described *Eileen's* cruise to Ireland in 1948 when everyone at home was experiencing rationing and many foods and luxuries could not be had for love or money. One reason for the voyage was to bring back as much as possible consistent with what the customs allowed. Bottles of whisky and gin, hams and other foods and even toy train sets were packed aboard much to the delight of those at home.

Bill did not keep his yachts for long in those days. He said his boats should always suit his circumstances at the time. As the family were growing up he and Edna felt *Eileen* was not really suitable for family cruising and decided to buy another yacht. This new boat was completely different A fine all teak gaff ketch of 50 ft on deck and 30 tons, *Ron* was designed by J.A. McCallum, and built by Robertsons of Sandbank in 1928. Her first owner was the very experienced yachtsman Colonel Charles Spencer, a former commodore of the Clyde Cruising Club. He also wrote a book called *Knots, Splices and Fancywork* which is a classic on the subject. There was a lot of his fancy ropework aboard *Ron*. Colonel Spencer had previously owned two other *Ron's*; the name means seal in Gaelic but this was the final development of his ideal cruising yacht. She was specifically designed for comfortable cruising on the West Coast of Scotland. He spent 6 months every summer cruising alone with two paid hands exploring almost every anchorage on the coast and believed that no-one could visit them all in one lifetime. Although built completely in teak with no expense spared *Ron* had an iron keel which Colonel Spencer thought was better protection for the hull if she should hit rocks! *Ron* is still sailing today, now in Australia and called *Ron of Argyll*. It is a tribute to her builders that she is still in excellent condition and even winning classic yacht races after so many years.

When Bill and Edna bought *Ron* in 1949 she came complete with a skipper - John McArthur from Rothesay who stayed with the boat having skippered her for the previous owner Mr. Manclark. John was a wonderful asset and a great teacher. As children we learned many things from him and also of course from my father and Harold. Not many people have the advantage of having two professional seamen to show them the ropes at an early age. As well as learning to row and sail in the dinghy John also taught us to fish. He was a professional fisherman, working mainly at that time dredging for clams (scallops). He had many years of experience in large yachts during the summer months and had crewed in the 46 ton cutter *Pretty Polly* and the famous schooner *Westward*. John had also crewed in the six metre *Circe* with Herbert Thom in the Seawanhaka Cup challenge in the thirties. John McArthur became a good friend of the family and stayed on as skipper in several boats after *Ron*, eventually leaving to do other things in 1961. John recalled a passage to Ireland in the *Ron* leaving Port Bannatyne on a Friday night. My father and Harold were asleep below and John was steering her with both jackyard topsails set. She was reaching fast past the Holy Isle and he was alone on deck at the tiller. The wind was increasing and he wanted to get the topsails off but could not leave the tiller to rouse the others. He held grimly on for a few hours and *Ron* being such a powerful ship held her sail until at last Bill and Harold appeared on deck, apologising profusely for leaving John alone for so long. John was such a gentleman that he said nothing but gratefully went to his bunk after stowing both topsails.

Gaff Ketch Ron

    Ron was a great yacht and my father was very fond of her but one day something happened which caused him to change direction again. My sister Joyce aged about 3 was holding the mainsheet horse which was just aft of the main hatch when going about one day. The heavy block and shackle just missed her fingers and my parents decided there and then to get a boat more suitable for young children. This resulted in the purchase of a 36 foot McCallum designed motor yacht called *Marie Rose*. I do not think my father was really happy with this but as he said at the time, "She will do for a few years until the children are old enough to go back to sail." John and Harold got on well and John was an expert with the splash net. This method of catching sea trout and salmon in the sea at night was only legal where a permit was held. John had a permit for the shores of Bute but there were times when the galley had a pile of sea trout which had mysteriously arrived aboard during the night! As I said we learned many things from John.

After two seasons, Bill decided to build a new boat. He had always admired the Scottish fishing boats and a few yachts on these lines had been built. *Scarbh, Earraid* and *Melfort* (formerly *Golden Beam*) were three examples of the type and he commissioned Bill McPherson Campbell to design a forty foot boat as a rugged family cruiser. The new yacht was to be built by Noble's of Girvan the well known fishing boat builders. *Tunnag* (Gaelic for duck) was heavily built in larch on oak with a Kelvin diesel engine. Although she was ketch rigged, the sails were really steadying sails, as *Tunnag* was primarily a motor vessel. It was a great advantage to be able to make a passage at 8 knots as young children always want to get ashore at the next anchorage. My sister Joyce aged 6 broke the bottle over *Tunnag's* bow at Noble's yard in the month of the Queen's Coronation in 1953. We had many happy holidays aboard, and whenever a sandy beach could be seen from afar, Joyce would appear on deck in her swimming costume and ask us to anchor! Bill had become vice commodore of the Clyde Cruising Club by then and *Tunnag* often served as the committee vessel for races.

The Clyde Cruising Club is Scotland's largest yacht club with around 2,200 members, and although without premises, which keep subscriptions at a modest level, most cruising and racing yachts in Scotland can fly the burgee. To digress for a moment, it is a mystery to me why so few yachts fly their club burgees nowadays. Some make the excuse that it is because of instruments and aerials etc. at the masthead but I don't buy that. Many classic yachts with the same equipment proudly fly their burgees and I think it is simply ignorance and a misplaced sense of fashion which has brought this about. Flag etiquette demands that the club burgee must be flown from the main mast head. Many yachts if they fly it at all; wrongly hoist it to the crosstrees which should be reserved for signals and courtesy flags.

The C.C.C. was formed in 1909 when a few young men agreed to found a yacht club purely for the cruising yachtsman. My wife Vivien's grandfather Douglas Lang once described the inauguration muster to me which he attended as a crew member of *Magic* a 4 ton Fife cutter, owned by one of the founders Murray Blair. The event was held at Colintraive and the newly appointed vice commodore Baillie Roderick Scott in his large schooner the *Ayacanora* invited all participants to dinner in a marquee pitched in the field opposite the Colintraive hotel. Over 40 yachts and some 130 members and friends attended and the evening was a great success. In those days most of the club yachts were much smaller than those of today, the *Ayacanora* being a notable exception. The club grew and prospered, organising many cruising and racing events over the years and in more recent times the Scottish racing series at Tarbert Loch Fyne currently sponsored by stockbrokers Bell Lawrie, one of the largest racing events in the U.K. Perhaps the club's greatest success is their sailing directions for the Scottish west coast which was compiled and updated by club members. It is still the best pilot book for yachtsmen in these waters. The club's aim is "to foster the social side of sailing" and some took this very much to heart as Douglas Lang recalled the scenes after the party at Colintraive with some waking up the next morning on the shore! Murray Blair penned a poem about the event, this is the last verse:-

> *When I awoke upon the shore,*
> *The water lapping at my shoes,*
> *I thought, as I had done before,*
> *Upon the awful curse of booze;*
> *Some thoughts came rifting through my head,*
> *Brought mayhap by the flowing tide,*
> *'Twas something the chairman said,*
> *'Bout fostering the social side!*

The C.C.C. has a club song; you will find the words in the appendix:

We made a few lengthy cruises in those years. The most notable being a cruise in 1956 to the Orkneys, round the North to the Caledonian Canal and back to the Clyde via the Crinan Canal. On arriving in Inverness, we met a German yacht from Bremen named *Senta*. They were on a passage round Britain and had diverted to Inverness as they had experienced very bad weather in the North Sea and needed to "lick their wounds". *Senta* was a 54ft wishbone ketch. This is an unusual but very effective rig which is described in detail later in this book. She had torn sails and the motor was out of action. Harold Brown in his usual way got chatting to her crew and Bill invited the owner Rolf Schmidt aboard *Tunnag*. As the evening wore on and after a few whiskies he agreed to tow *Senta* through the canal. This was the start of a life long friendship. We towed them not only through the Caledonian Canal, but also through the Crinan Canal where we left them to sail home south through the Irish Sea and the English Channel.

This friendship gave me the opportunity to go to Bremen on an exchange with Heiko, Rolf's eldest son the following year. I sailed with the family in *Senta* in Denmark and Heiko sailed with my family in *Northward*. You can read more of this in chapter 3.

Tunnag

Chapter 2 - Learning to Sail

In 1957 Bill had itchy feet again and decided it was time to go back to sail. As youngsters Kenneth and I were keen to learn how to sail properly and the next boat was *Northward*. A Milne design built by McGruer in 1930, *Northward* was the largest yacht McGruer's had built at that time. 20 tons T.M. 50 foot overall and 35 foot on the waterline she was the optimum size for family cruising and handicap racing. *Northward* was rigged as a bermudan sloop with a very large mainsail and small jib. This could be a handful particularly as there was no standing backstay. Support of the mast relied on the runners! We continued to cruise as a family every year on the west coast as was our custom and in 1959 *Senta* came over again from Bremen to cruise in company with us. Both yachts took part in the C.C.C. Tobermory race and sailed north to Skye and the outer isles. Donald McIntyre from Port Bannatyne crewed in the *Senta* to provide local knowledge which he found a most interesting experience. One amusing incident was when anyone up early one morning in Tobermory would have seen the startling sight of Rolf Schmidt standing stark naked on the deck of *Senta*, with one of his boys throwing buckets of cold sea water over him. Rugged types these Germans!

At Skye we anchored in Loch Scavaig which is a remote, sheltered but bleak anchorage under the Cuillin Mountains. We were mesmerised by the sight of hundreds of sea trout jumping all around the boat but John McArthur knew that the gamekeepers were watching every yacht. There were even iron hooks fixed to the bottom near the burn to catch illegal nets. We decided to visit Lachie Robertson who was a teacher at Glasgow Academy but hailed from Elgol the nearest village. Lachie was my class teacher at that time! We got him aboard and soon the drams were flowing. We discovered that the head gamekeeper was Lachie's cousin, so before long he had joined the party along with his assistant. Time went by and as we poured them into the dinghy to go ashore after midnight, the head gamekeeper said "chust do what you like boys, I'm going to bed!" With no more ado, the net was put into the dinghy and after a few shots across the burn we had a total of 120 sea trout. No big ones, all were under 1 ½ pounds but I have never seen so many before or since! Standing on the footbridge over the burn which runs from Loch Coruisk to the sea, you could not see the bottom for the solid mass of fish making their way up to the loch. The Germans were amazed and as we had so many sea trout we distributed them amongst the yachts in the anchorage. We still had some left over when we arrived in Mallaig the next day and had to look for people to give them to! I now know why there was once a local by law in Glasgow prohibiting householders from giving their servants salmon more than three times a week!

Northward with original sloop rig

Northward was in many ways an ideal family cruiser but the large mainsail was a problem. The boom was over 30 feet long and we had a few difficult times reefing. Bill in his habitual way decided to get a more manageable boat and John McArthur also decided to do other things. *Northward* was put on the market in 1961 and *Aeolian* was bought. She was a Robert Clark 12 ton yawl and we had her for just one season. In reality *Aeolian* was just too small for our family needs. We were at an age when we wanted to take our friends sailing but with the family and Harold there was just not enough room and she was sold to Dr. Spiers in Stornoway. Many years later *Aeolian* was wrecked with the loss of two lives on the east coast of England which was a great tragedy. Her owner had an exact replica built in 1994 at the International Boat Building College in Lowestoft.

As *Northward* had not yet been sold, Dad discussed the possibility of converting her to ketch rig with Bill Campbell who had designed *Tunnag*. This seemed to be the ideal solution. We were all very fond of her and she was in many ways ideal for us, but her rig and accommodation could be improved to make her more suitable for family sailing. Morris and Lorimer's yard at Sandbank made a new mizzen mast and moved the galley from the forecastle to a new position aft on the starboard side. This allowed for four berths in the forecastle in place of the old galley. The owner's cabin on the port side became a double cabin and altogether we now had nine berths. Kenneth, Joyce and I soon took advantage of this and many of our friends came sailing with us, some experienced and some not so! We could always tell as soon as a newcomer stepped into the dinghy if they would be any good aboard or not. Unfortunately some of the keenest were the most useless! I remember once my mother on clearing the table after lunch, asking a young friend of Kenneth's to shake the crumbs from the tablecloth overboard. Believe it or not, he threw the whole cloth over the side and thought that is what he was supposed to do!

With the new ketch rig we were keen to go further afield and a cruise to Southern Ireland was planned for 1962. We always started our holidays on the Glasgow Fair Friday, that being the main holiday weekend. We made a fast passage to Dunlaogaire where we sampled the Guinness and visited the three yacht clubs – Royal Irish, Royal St. George and the National. We were royally looked after and the older generation spent much time with old friends including the well known Irish yachtsman Billy Mooney, while we youngsters explored the town. We then sailed south, calling at Arklow, Wicklow and Dunmore East where we met with *Cruinnaig III*, George Christie's fine varnished ketch also from the Clyde. We had a great time with his family and cruised in company for a few days. We called at various harbours as far west as Schull and sailed out to the Fastnet rock. One night at Kinsale we had a meal at a restaurant called "The Spinnaker". There was a litter of Siamese kittens there and Joyce looked at her father with her pleee-ase daddy look and somehow we had a kitten on board! She was duly named "Tiki" and adapted remarkably quickly to life at sea. On arrival home at Port Bannatyne "Tiki" was hidden in a locker away from the customs officer's eyes but while clearing us and having a dram she mewed loudly and he asked how a cat managed living aboard. Fortunately he did not ask where she had come from.

Northward with ketch rig

I took part in the Mudhook Schools and Universities regatta for a few years. This event is organised by the Mudhook Yacht Club for students of schools and universities from all over the U.K. Owners of Dragons and Gareloch One Designs kindly lent their boats for the week with a "caretaker" aboard to keep an eye on things. This regatta is very popular with students and the Mudhook still organise it, providing many young people with their first experience of keelboat racing. Our team from Glasgow Academy did not do very well but we had a lot of fun, particulary in getting to know some wild Irishmen from Queen's College Belfast. "Winkie" Nixon became a friend, and was one of the wildest; in a good humoured way not aggressively or vandalistic as some are today. He and his crew Colm McLafferty and Ed Wheeler were first class sailors and won the week but they were always up to high jinks. The race organisers were rather stiff and pompous and Winkie and his crew arrived on the jetty each morning dressed in the most peculiar clothes with long hair and a large alarm clock round Colm's neck as a stop watch. Winkie had just got back from circumnavigating Ireland with Colm in an 18 foot Waverley class dayboat. The story goes that he did not tell his parents but bought supplies from the local grocer in Bangor, charging them to his father's account and sailed off in the legitimately borrowed boat! They made the voyage successfully sleeping on the floorboards when not steering and even had tea with the lighthouse keeper on the Fastnet Rock!

The following year Dad agreed with Rolf Schmidt of *Senta* that we would sail to Norway where we would all meet up. I had been working in Bremen and by then spoke reasonable German. Kenneth and I along with Harold, John Carmichael and Frithjof, one of Rolf Schmidt's sons took *Northward* up to Inverness through the canal ready for the passage to Norway. Colin McPhail with my father, mother and Joyce arrived and we had an uneventful passage across to Stavanger. We cruised northwards up the Norwegian coast visiting Hardanger Fiord, Sogne Fiord and Bergen as well as some of the offshore islands. It is certainly a wonderful and spectacular cruising ground and sailing in a fiord with mountains rising thousands of feet from the sea and to see glaciers high above on the mountain slopes is a strange experience. We had to be careful to watch for sudden down draughts and squalls when under sail. Our cruise in company with *Senta* and our German friends was successful but for one incident. It was noticeable that when tied up alongside if we were next to the quay people would come to talk to us but in one port when *Senta* was alongside we were both ignored. Feelings in Norway about the war were still raw 15 years later. Some Norwegians could not understand why we had Germans as friends.

Wishbone ketch Senta

We left *Senta* and set off for home. The weather had deteriorated giving us a stormy but fast passage across the North Sea. The ketch rig had proved itself as we could reduce sail easily by handing either the mizzen or mainsail. By the time we reached the Scottish coast the wind and sea had died down and we had a pleasant sail through the Pentland Firth across the Minch to Stornoway where we met old friends. Charlie Morrison a business friend of my father took charge and showed us some real highland hospitality. I am sure we visited every drinking den on Lewis and heard some very funny stories. Charlie was a real character who seemed to know everyone on the island and we eventually we got everyone back on board and set off across the Minch for home waters again.

At this time Kenneth and I spent some time at the Clyde Cruising Club's dinghy section at Bardowie Loch near Glasgow. We also sailed our yacht tender which Dad had fitted with sails and centreboard for us. As we became older my father bought an old Dragon class yacht named *Todday* after the fictional island in "Whisky Galore". This was to get us properly involved in racing and as this was our first yacht, we were really proud of her. We had many good days and a few mishaps. One of these was before the start at Shandon in the Gareloch one evening. We were concentrating on looking ashore for the starting signals, when suddenly there was a tremendous crash as *Todday* smacked right into an Admiralty mooring buoy! What a shock! Dad was not happy, but the damage was repaired by McGruer on the insurance by the next week. Another incident was more spectacular. We had entered the Dragon Gold Cup regatta at Rothesay where Dragons from all over the world had gathered. We were not doing very well and one day when running under spinnaker in a fresh breeze we were heading for the lee mark off Toward Point, as most of the fleet were beating towards us in the opposite direction. I was at the helm and I thought everything was clear, when suddenly a bow appeared seemingly from nowhere under our lee on the port side. This was followed by a piercing female scream and the crash of breaking timber. One of the leading boats on starboard tack had crashed into us. The bow went right over our port quarter, fortunately missing our heads by inches, caught on our backstay and caused us to gybe all standing. The mast stood up and as we cleared away the wreckage, the other boat was lying to our lee. I looked up the sail number on the race programme to discover that she belonged to none other than Princess Sophia of Greece, now the Queen of Spain! We shouted an apology as we were in the wrong by the rules and limped to Port Bannatyne for repairs. In the evening at the function in the Glenburn Hotel I went to the princess and offered my apologies. She was very gracious and said she had tacked and simply did not see us under her genoa. She said in my defence that I had obviously not seen her on starboard tack as she hit us very soon after going about. Previously my family's only contact with royalty was at the Royal Clyde Yacht Club Centenary Regatta in 1956 at Rothesay, when my father was vice commodore of the C.C.C. He and my mother, along with the other clubs' flag officers were invited to a reception aboard *Britannia* where they were introduced to the Duke of Edinburgh. I think my introduction to royalty was more unusual!

After a few years it became obvious that *Todday* was outclassed by newer and more expensive boats, so we sold her and bought a Gareloch One Design called *Catriona*. The Gareloch class continues to race to this day and recently celebrated their 80th anniversary with most of the original boats in commission. They were designed and built by McGruer of Clynder in 1924, and although many of the boats had migrated south to Aldeburgh in the fifties, John Henderson of Rhu had managed to get all 16 boats back on the Clyde in time for their 40th anniversary regatta in the Gareloch in 1964 which we took part in with *Catriona*. The big advantage of one design boats is that as they are all virtually identical, prizewinning is achieved by skill rather than chequebook. The class even orders new sails for the whole class from one sailmaker at one time, drawing lots to ensure equality. The Garelochs have provided excellent low cost racing for young and old for all those years, which was much more to our liking as by now Kenneth and I had to pay for the boat ourselves. My father still had *Northward* and went by steamer to Port Bannatyne on Friday evenings for weekends where she was moored, returning home on Sunday nights. We raced on Tuesday and Thursday evenings in *Catriona* and back aboard *Northward* again on Fridays. It was all great fun and no doubt kept us from some of the less healthy activities which many young people got up to in the sixties.

Thalia (4) and Catriona (3) Gareloch class

We took part in many races in *Northward*. These were mainly Clyde Cruising Club events and we were reasonably successful. The main annual event was the Tobermory Race which at its peak had over 150 entries. The race started on Glasgow Fair Friday in mid July when the fleet gathered at Port Bannatyne for the early Saturday morning start. The course was through the Kyles of Bute, round Ardlamont Point into Loch Fyne and finishing at Ardrishaig. The yachts then made their way through the Crinan Canal as soon as they arrived at Ardrishaig or on the Sunday to gather at Crinan for the next leg to Tobermory. With such a large fleet the organisation was sometimes stretched and club officials had worried looks on their faces for most of the weekend. In spite of some overcrowding in the locks, engine breakdowns and crews disappearing at Cairnbaan to the pub; somehow all the boats managed to be either in the canal basin or anchored off Crinan by the Sunday evening. There was always a great atmosphere and it was like the start of a great adventure. Many boats had families aboard and most of them made this the start of their annual cruise. We were no exception and it was always with anticipation that we came through the sea lock at Crinan to get ready for the race the next morning.

The time of the start of the race from Crinan to Tobermory was always governed by the tide. The start had to be at low water to take advantage of the north-flowing flood tide through the Dorus Mor and Pladda. This means that in some years the race could start as early as 4.00 AM and many crews did not go to bed at all. Parties aboard often followed a riotous evening ashore and Nick Ryan of the Crinan Hotel despaired of some of his young customers and their antics. I remember a young relative of mine being barred from the hotel for pouring beer from the rooftop bar onto the crowd below. A great time was had by all except of course the mothers with young children who were trying vainly to get them to go to sleep, but when dawn broke and the yachts started to weigh anchor and get underway, bleary eyed crews hauled on anchor chains, halyards and sheets waiting for the race committee to fire the starting gun from the battlements in front of the hotel. Then they were off; a flurry of boats all trying to find the best position for the start in a quite restricted area between the Dubh rock and the shore. Often some unfortunate would go aground on an unmarked rock to add to the entertainment.

On through the Dorus Mor and if the wind held the fleet gradually spread out. I remember one year the yachts all came together in a calm early in the morning between Scarba and Luing. We were sucked through the sound on the tide and as the sun was rising, someone started to play music. Soon others joined in and accordion, guitar and even bagpipes contributed to a wonderful atmosphere with the red sun rising over the hills. It did not last long though, as the wind came up and the impromptu concert was over. The wind was from astern and the bigger boats soon pulled ahead under spinnakers. By the time we reached Duart Castle at the entrance to the Sound of Mull the first boats were well away up the Sound and we in *Northward* were amongst them. As always in these waters the weather can never be taken for granted and often the wind would fall and the fleet would come together again. The first boat home at Tobermory received a bottle of Old Mull whisky from the Western Isles Yacht Club and prizes were awarded on handicap by the C.C.C. The celebrations at Tobermory usually went on for a couple of days before the yachts dispersed. Many went north to explore the islands and some sailed home via Crinan or round the Mull of Kintyre.

One year in Tobermory Kenneth, Joyce and I along with our friends Peter and Sandy Nicolson were at the Saturday night dance in the Aros Hall where the boys and girls lined up on opposite sides of the hall; the girls waiting patiently to be asked to dance, with some of the local boys secretly drinking from hidden quarter bottles in their pockets. Bobby McLeod and his band often played at these dances and I have fond memories of that time. At the end of the evening the boys who had picked up a girl always took her home. Kenneth had the misfortune to choose a girl from Salen which is a good few miles from Tobermory and eventually got back aboard at dawn. Peter, Sandy and I could not find Joyce but decided to go back aboard anyway. We thought we were very clever as we tried to silently descend the fore hatch but suddenly my father boomed from his bunk in the saloon. "What is going on? Are you all aboard? PRESENT YOURSELVES!!!!!" I explained that Kenneth had been delayed but unfortunately I did not know where Joyce was. This was a mistake and before he responded Sandy said she had "got off" with one of the divers from the Tobermory Galleon diving ship. My mother tried vainly to calm my father down and you could cut the tension with a knife. Fortunately Joyce appeared shortly afterwards and we all got a little sleep to be awakened later by Kenneth's return from Salen.

Sadly the Tobermory Race is no longer such a big event. It is still on the C.C.C. calendar but numbers are no longer so great. Fewer families now make this the start of their West Coast holiday as fashions change and young people want to do their own thing at ever earlier ages. Although the Clyde yachting scene has greatly changed over my lifetime a few boats have been in the same hands for many years. I think of *Boomerang* an 8 ton Laurent Giles Brittany class boat which is owned by Frank and Katie Christie. Katie's father Harry McLean built her in his yard at Renfrew in 1955. Katie inherited her and still cruises regularly. Another is Mrs Jean Keppie whose late husband built *Trefoil* a Mylne 7 tonner in 1950 and only recently gave up sailing after over 50 years! Douglas Steedman owner of *Ivanhoe* a 9 ton Nicholson sloop has taken part in every Tobermory race for at least 30 years, perhaps longer as I have lost count!

Our early training by John McArthur was not forgotten, both in sailing and in fishing. He had taught me to be a reasonable helmsman and I was always fishing or looking for opportunities to set our lobster creels or long lines. I remember we once caught a large lobster in our creel just east of Tobermory pier. John, Harold and of course my father's influence gave me a wonderful start to a lifelong hobby and interest and I will always be thankful to my parents who made it possible.

Northward was sold in 1969 as Kenneth and I had bought the 8 Metre *Wye*. My father replaced *Northward* with a 12 ton Hillyard called *Romeiro* which was more suitable for my parents and Harold to cruise in. The new owner of *Northward* had ambitious plans to sail her south to the sun but sadly this changed abruptly. When sailing single handed in calm weather one night in the English Channel off Portland Bill, he went below to light the kettle. As soon as he struck the match there was a tremendous explosion and he was thrown out of the hatch hitting the mizzen mast and landing in the water a few yards from the yacht. He watched horrified as flames rapidly spread from the hatch and *Northward* slowly sank as she burned to the waterline. Fortunately the dinghy was being towed and he managed to swim to it and climb aboard, getting clear just before *Northward* disappeared below the sea. He was later picked up by a fishing boat. A sad end to a fine yacht but at least the owner escaped due to the dinghy. What a dreadful experience for any yachtsman and one which we should all learn from. Since then I have always been very careful about gas and fire aboard. This poem was written by Cecil Day Lewis the Poet Laureate at the time and a friend of *Northward's* first owner. It hung on the saloon bulkhead all her days.

The Northward

Under a hillside by sunny Gareloch
Scaring the Cormorant off his wave perch, floated
Forth on the springtime into my element.
I, the yacht Northward.

Seven brothers built my body of oak and elm,
Woke in the dumb wood a spirit seafaring,
Hoisted the spruce tree to command a new world
Silent of bird voice

None is so beautiful, whether undaunted
Flaunt I my colours close to the wild wind's eye,
Or cleaving calm seas, gold on my spinnaker,
Dream down the evening.

Men say, who sight me naked on the pure sky,
Surely such craft once carried in his flame-spun
Pall, a dead Viking past the horizon
Into Valhalla.

Land's End to Lewis I know, but I love best
My western islands where the rain purrs on
Blue profound anchorage, where the moon climbs
Over the Cuillins

When you are done with me. Let me still be happy,
Wrap my ribs deep in tides Hebridean.
And for a riding light, clear above me,
Set the Aurora.

The Northward by Cecil Day Lewis (Copyright 8 The Estate of C. Day-Lewis 1930) is reproduced by permission of PFD (www.pfd.co.uk) on behalf of the Estate of C. Day-Lewis

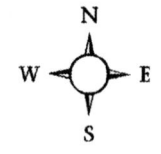

Chapter 3 - The German Connection

In chapter 1, I told the story of our meeting the Schmidt family in *Senta* in 1955. This started a chain of events which had a significant influence on my life. Rolf Schmidt and my father agreed that it would benefit their eldest sons to exchange places for a summer. I was sent to Bremen and Heiko came to Scotland for six weeks. I had been sent to the Berlitz school of languages after school twice a week to learn some German as my father was determined that I should learn the language. On arriving at the Schmidt's lovely house overlooking the river Lesum outside Bremen, I was told that his four boys Heiko, Ingolf, Frithjof and Holger would only speak German to me! This was quite a shock but I quite soon began to understand them and after Heiko flew to Scotland to be with my family I spent much time with Ingolf who was slightly older than me and Frithjof who was a little younger. We rode bikes, raced dinghies and sailed on *Senta* at weekends. *Senta* was moored at the yacht club in the river Lesum, a tributary of the Weser but compared to the Clyde the sailing water was very restricted. It was a long sail down the river Weser to the sea, a bit like keeping your yacht in Glasgow and sailing down the river at weekends. Once you got to the sea there was only Bremerhaven which is a major port or Heligoland (or Helgoland in German) the island 28 miles out in the North sea. We are certainly spoiled in Scotland.

Heligoland is an interesting place. A rocky island only one mile long of distinctive red rock cliffs, It stands out on the North Sea as a guardian of the North German coast. The island was British from 1807 to 1890 when it became German in exchange for Zanzibar. The community flourishes principally from fishing and tourism. Crowds of tourists come every day in the summer from Bremerhaven and Cuxhaven to take advantage of the island's duty free status. The shops are crammed with duty free goods - tobacco, alcohol, cameras and almost everything else and the island's streets are packed with noisy holidaymakers when the boats are in. As there are few alternative harbours on the German coast, many yachtsmen sail to Heligoland for the weekend. There is a fine marina now but when I was there we tied up in the main harbour and local lobster with Sekt (German sparkling wine) was obligatory aboard *Senta*. The neighbouring sandy island Dunen has a nudist beach which is always packed with sun seekers in the summer months.

In July *Senta* sailed for Denmark through the Kiel Canal into the Baltic. I would now like to tell you about this fine vessel. *Senta* is 54 feet (16m) overall. She was designed by Max Oertz as a gaff ketch, and built at the Deutsche Werft in Keil in 1928. In 1933 Heinrich Schmidt, Rolf Schmidt's father bought her and in 1936 converted her to the wishbone ketch rig she has today. He was impressed by this unusual rig which yacht builders Abeking and Rasmussen in Bremen and Uffa Fox the English designer had pioneered. The rig has a conventional mizzen and headsails but the space between the masts is filled with two sails. A boomed staysail from the head of the mizzen mast to the foot of the main, and a triangular mainsail with the clew sheeted to the head of the mizzen mast with the characteristic "wishbone" gaff which is a curved spar similar in shape to the boom on a windsurfer. This spar allows greater control of the sail and allows it to spread well downwind. For some reason the rig never really caught on and *Senta* is one of the very few yachts anywhere in the world to carry it. Critics had denounced the wishbone as top heavy or unseamanlike but the Schmidts' experience is very different. In 69 years racing and cruising, including many long distance voyages there has never been a problem with the rig. The sheeting position to the head of the mizzen means that instant control of the wishbone is easily made from the cockpit. When wind increases the first "reef" is to drop the mainsail reducing sail where it matters, high up then the boat is then well balanced under main staysail, headsails and mizzen. (see illustration)

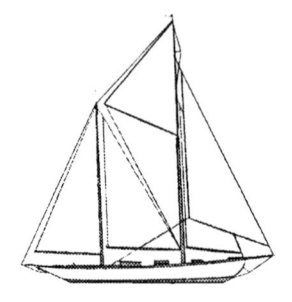

Senta's sailplan

This rig has many advantages for short handed cruising. It is however essential that the mizzen mast is strong enough and adequately stayed to take the load of the wishbone gaff and mainsail loading, a permanent backstay is essential. Perhaps some of the problems others have experienced were due to inadequate rigging or mast specifications.

To get back to my Danish cruise. The crew were Rolf and Inge Schmidt along with three of their sons - Ingolf, Frithjof and Holger. There was also Egon Lindhorst their skipper and myself. We sailed from the river Weser to Heligoland then on to Brunsbuttel at the west end of the 50 mile Kiel Canal. We made the passage through the canal in one day and arrived at Holtenau, the Baltic end of the canal. We spent two happy weeks exploring the Danish islands visiting Aeroskoping, Svendborg, Middelfart, Assens and Sonderburg, sailing round the island of Foen. In those days there were far fewer yachts in these waters and at the island of Langoere we were anchored with only one other yacht. Today I hear that it is hard to find a place to tie up or anchor. I had one remarkable co-incidence. In Sonderburg we were tied up alongside another German yacht from Hamburg when we discovered that they also had a British person aboard. This was a girl who turned out to be the niece of my music teacher back in Glasgow! It's a small world right enough!

During the cruise I had been dropped in at the deep end as far as the language was concerned but I surprised myself by soon being able to understand and communicate with the others in German. It is a fact that if one is exposed to a foreign language at an early age it is amazing how quickly one learns, as a young person's brain absorbs information like a sponge. This was to prove invaluable to me in future years. I got on well with the Schmidt boys but one incident was amusing in hindsight but not so funny at the time. I had been cheeky to Egon, so he along with Ingolf thought it would be funny to tie me to the mast when they went ashore. This was alongside the quay at a place rejoicing in the name of Middelfart where I suffered the humility of passers-by looking at me, nodding their heads or laughing. They let me go after half an hour when they came back aboard. Such is the Teutonic sense of humour!

The Senta crew for the Baltic cruise

I was only 14 years old when I first went to Bremen but Rolf Schmidt had an acquaintance, Heinrich Lerbs who had the same type of ironmongery and hardware business as my father. Five years later when I was 19, he arranged for me to spend six months working there while Mr Lerbs' son Hinnerk came to Glasgow to work in our firm. This was quite daunting and at the same time exciting. My father's view was that as I was too young to have been called up for National Service, he wanted me to experience working away from home for a while and learn a language into the bargain. He was very far sighted, as he said we would probably be in the Common Market before long, and languages would be important for business. He had spent a few months in Germany as a young man and thought his friendship with Rolf Schmidt was a wonderful opportunity for me and later my brother Kenneth. In Bremen I soon got into the way of life and made many new friends. During my time there I sailed with the S.K.W.B. yacht club where Rolf Schmidt was commodore. The club owned two yachts at that time, *Roland von Bremen* and *Wappen von Bremen*. Both were quite elderly but the club's function at that time was not racing but to take young people to sea and train them, rather like our R.Y.A. courses. Each yacht was skippered by an experienced club member and youngsters were awarded certificates at different stages of their sea training. Neither

Roland nor *Wappen* had engines and a high standard of seamanship was expected and practiced. The yachts travelled long distances and each year at least one blue water cruise was made. This could be round the British Isles as *Senta* in the year we met, or south to the Azores or north to Iceland. Many sea miles were covered by the S.K.W.B. boats. The club still functions as described but now with newer and larger yachts. These are funded by charitable donations and sponsorship and club yachts have taken part in the Whitbread and other major ocean racing events.

 I remember one weekend cruise aboard the *Wappen von Bremen* in a cold February with a hard frost at night. We cruised to Heligoland and there was one complete novice on board. The poor boy had come aboard with all his brand new sailing gear, including a yachting cap and had overindulged in the schnapps and beer on the first night aboard. We were all wakened to the sound and smell of him vomiting over the whole cabin at 3.00 AM. The skipper was furious and not just the skipper! He was dragged on deck in the freezing cold, stripped off and buckets of freezing water thrown over him. This was a lesson which I am sure he never forgot. I don't know if he ever went sailing again but I expect he drank less at least for a while. I recall another time in Heligoland when I was persuaded to play my accordion at a party aboard. Everyone was in great form and late at night we all thought it was a good idea to go ashore. I was persuaded to bring the accordion along and I accompanied drunken singing along the main street. Someone found a wheelbarrow and sat me in it as I played. Suddenly two policemen arrived and stopped us. My friends all disappeared into the night leaving me sitting in the barrow with my accordion. Fortunately I had not been completely deserted. My friend Hans Seyde who shares my birthday whispered "Don't say a word in German, I'll deal with this" As Hans was a law student I assumed he might know how to handle the situation. We were however taken to the police station and left in a cell until the morning. This was the cause of much hilarity for the rest of my time in Bremen.

 The winter of 1962 was one of the coldest of the century and in Bremen we had lots of snow and ice. So much so, that the flat land outside Bremen which had flooded was frozen solid for a few weeks and everyone took up skating. You could literally skate for miles taking care to avoid wire fences and other obstacles. Herr Lerbs had a share in a small coaster called *Ceres* and arranged for his son Hinnerk and I to go on a passage to Stockholm. I was quite excited as I had not sailed in a commercial vessel before. We sailed from Bremen, through the Kiel Canal and to my surprise we found the Baltic completely frozen on our way north to Stockholm. We followed an icebreaker through as the ice was very thick and passed people walking or even driving cars a few miles offshore. The temperature was minus 30 at one point but the ship was warm and we had a few laughs with the crew. As we approached Stockholm, there was great activity as everyone seemed to be buying duty frees from the second mate who had opened the "shop". I was asked if I wanted anything but saw little point as I had all I wanted aboard. I then noticed that most of the crew were buying cheap schnapps which was like firewater! Hinnerk and I were puzzled until we tied up in the dock. No sooner had our lines touched the quay when a dozen or so scruffy individuals rushed up to us and scrambled aboard. Swift exchanges of Swedish Kroner for bottles of schnapps ensued and the men disappeared back into the shadows of the dock sheds as quickly as they had come. A few minutes later the customs arrived to clear us and of course no-one had anything to declare! It appeared that this practice was tolerated in Sweden as alcoholics and down and outs congregate in the docks waiting for foreign ships, as alcohol was and still is very expensive in Sweden. It was disturbing to see how the crews profiteered from these people. A bottle of schnapps which cost less than 2 marks aboard duty free was sold for about 10 times that amount, with similar margins on cigarettes. This of course was to finance the crews' high living ashore. We went with other crew members to various haunts to discover that there were three grades of beer sold. Most places only sold the weak beer which was cheaper but dear by German standards. The better beer was only available in certain expensive clubs and restaurants which did not welcome sailors! There was not much to do in Stockholm at that time of year but we went to a dance where all the girls lined up on one side of the hall and the boys secretly slugged schnapps from hidden bottles – just like the dances at Tobermory or Tarbert! I eventually plucked up enough courage to ask a pretty Swedish blonde to dance to be met with a one word response "Ne", - a somewhat cold introduction to the inhabitants of a cold country! I have since visited Sweden several times and made friends with several Swedish people whom I have found without exception to be friendly and kind.

All in all, the experience of living and working in Germany was very worthwhile. I had learned the language well enough to be able to converse, read and write German reasonably well. I had experienced German business methods and customs. Above all I had learned about other people, different from my background in many ways but people with the same aspirations and fears as people in any part of the world. I strongly recommend that young people to try to find an opportunity to live abroad for a while, preferably where English is not spoken. Many continental families are keen to arrange exchanges with British youngsters and there are some organisations which facilitate these. After Germany I went on to work in Belgium and France but I had no sailing there except for an afternoon sail with some friends in a small boat in Holland.

Chapter 4 - International 8 metres

Yacht racing "The king of sports and the sport of kings" as someone once said. Certainly it is the sport of kings. King George V and other members of the Royal Family have been yachtsmen. The Queen and Prince Philip once owned the Nicholson yawl *Bloodhound* and Princess Anne owns a yacht which she sails with her husband on the west coast of Scotland. Apart from my incident with Princess Sophia of Greece and once shaking hands with the Queen at the Royal Northern Yacht Club's 150th anniversary I have had no other experience of royalty. I do however enjoy yacht racing and have been fortunate in having raced in several different classes as well as handicap racing over the years.

I started learning to race at Bardowie Loch in the old wooden dinghies they had in the fifties. I have few recollections of that time but I do remember helping to varnish the boats in the spring, learning the racing rules on a blackboard in the clubhouse and putting them into practice on the water. Collisions and capsizes were common and I remember the water was quite green, just like pea soup on occasions. Once Dad bought *Northward* I really got interested in racing. We had seen races starting and finishing many times before when *Tunnag* was the committee vessel but then I was more interested in my fishing rod than the finer points of the race. *Northward* with John McArthur was a completely new experience and Kenneth and I got keen and competitive. *Northward* was entered for every Clyde Cruising Club race starting with the Opening Muster at Hunter's Quay in May, finishing the season with the Closing Muster at Rothesay in September. She was reasonably fast and we won or were placed in many events including the Ailsa Craig and Tobermory races. We also raced over to Cultra in Belfast Lough. We never had a crewing problem as there were always plenty of our school friends keen to come. Some were first class but others were the "don't call us we'll call you" types – willing and keen but quite useless!

I had always admired the International 8 Metre boats and a few sailed regularly in the C.C.C. races. In the 1967 Tobermory race, the sight of these magnificent thoroughbreds crossing the line close together really excited us and Kenneth and I decided there and then that we wanted an 8 Metre. We knew that there were a few old 8's in Cork Harbour in the South of Ireland,

International 8 Metre Wye

We had seen them there a few years before. *If* had just been bought by Tommy Rose and was coming to the Clyde but *Wye* a 1935 Nicholson boat and *Severn II* a 1934 Milne design were still for sale. A visit to Cork found both boats laid up and we had the choice of either boat. We were most impressed with *Wye*. She was beautiful with an impossibly long Nicholson bow overhang, very similar to *Endeavour* the Nicholson J Class yacht built in their Gosport yard in the previous year 1934. *Wye* was also unaltered with her original rig. We just knew this was a special boat and we had to have her. We rapidly cleared out our savings and bought *Wye* for £2,900 from her Irish owner. We had arranged for the yard to do essential fitting out and at Easter 1968 we went back to Cork to bring her home.

The International 8 Metre Class started in 1906 and developed into a popular racing class being selected for the Olympic Games from 1908 to 1936. 8 Metre yachts are not 8 metres long but typically between 13 and 15 metres overall. The International Rating Rule which governs all the Metre boat classes, 5, 6, 7, 8, 9, 10, 12, 15, 19 and 23 metres are not measurements of the yacht's size in metres but a formula based on various dimensions to produce a rating. This rule enables boats with different measurements and hull shapes to race competitively together and although some of the differences between yachts of the same class can be significant, the rule is so well formulated that it is difficult to design a yacht to beat the rule. This has ensured the long racing life of the metre rule boats and its success was one of the reasons for its choice for the revival of the America's Cup. At the present time the 6 and 8 metre classes are both experiencing a revival. Classic metre yachts are prized and many have been restored at great expense by wealthy owners and several new boats have been built to take part in regattas held in various countries. The 8 metre class had been strong on the Clyde before the war but had gradually dispersed. As there was little interest in metre boats in the late sixties a few of us were able to buy vintage boats cheaply which gave us some wonderful racing.

Wye had no engine and her equipment was somewhat tired and worn out, so it was with some trepidation we set off for home. We had a good crew for the voyage. Kenneth and I, Tom Reid, Harold Jack, Winkie Nixon for local knowledge and Harold Brown as experienced navigator made up the ship's compliment. We had a famously hospitable leaving party hosted by Charlie Dwyer (Rear Admiral of the Royal Cork Yacht Club the oldest yacht club in the world) and his family at his house the night before and most of us were feeling somewhat fragile. We woke in the morning to a cold easterly wind but we were hopeful of enough south in it to enable us to fetch along the Irish coast. On leaving the relative calm of Cork harbour we found a brisk easterly breeze outside with a lumpy sea that soon had most of our heads in buckets or over the side. Our original intention was to keep going until we had reached the east coast, but as were becoming very cold and tired with all the windward work, we decided to stop at Dunmore East to catch up on our sleep. It was dark when we approached the harbour and under reduced sail we anxiously looked for the harbour lights as shown on the chart. Once I was sure we had identified them we turned in towards the lights and assumed we were on course for Dunmore East harbour. We were reaching in with the wind on the starboard quarter and as we came closer suddenly Winkie shouted "Luff up! Get out of here – breakers ahead!" He heard the noise of seas breaking on the sandy beach of Tramore Bay just west of Dunmore East. I was at the helm and immediately luffed and tacked out to sea again. Thanks to Winkie's keen hearing we were saved from disaster. We studied the chart again and again and sailed further east until eventually we were sure of the correct harbour lights. We slipped in and tied up alongside a fishing boat. We all slept well that night but I had nightmares for weeks afterwards about our near miss and learned the lesson of never sailing into a lee shore at night until you really know for sure where you are.

The next day we dried out, cleaned ship and made minor repairs. While sewing slides onto our heavy cut down cruising mainsail which we had decided was more suitable for passage making than our best racing one, Harold Jack who was a novice to sailing unfortunately stepped on the sail which was spread over a neighbouring fishing boat hatch and broke his wrist thus ending his passage. I suspect he was a little relieved to be missing the Irish Sea and as far as I know he never sailed again. In the afternoon the lifeboat maroon went off and the fishing boat alongside suddenly cast us off to answer the call, which was a capsized dinghy. The fishing boat aided by the local lifeboat picked up the dinghy crew, watched by it seemed, the whole of the population of Dunmore East as we were left drifting engineless across the harbour. Thanks to Kenneth's skill with a heaving line gained from many passages through the Crinan Canal, we soon got a warp ashore and all was well.

On leaving Dunmore East I was concerned about the unsettled weather but we decided to push on and get north as quickly as possible. The temperature and the glass had risen and although still easterly we had a pleasant beat to the south east corner of Ireland. Visibility was poor and we decided to keep offshore and go out to the Conningbeg Light Vessel before beating in a falling wind against the ebb to Carnsore Point. The Barrels Light Ship came out of the mist so we had a good fix of our position and as the visibility improved we crawled inshore to avoid the tide. We made our way through Tuskar Sound although we never saw the Tuskar rock causing our deep sea navigator Harold some concern about our "rock crawling". The tide turned and with a light easterly and the tide under us we had a wonderful sail up the Irish Sea. Off Wicklow Head the wind died away again and for a while we drifted in the mist and rain, but soon the easterly came away stronger and we tramped along with two stormy petrels for company. Suddenly there was a loud bang as the jib halyard parted and gale warnings came over the radio. A jib sheet lead also flew off the deck as the fixing bolts gave way. I was now concerned about the gear as we knew the boat needed to be properly overhauled.

It was time to find a port, so we turned back to Dunlaoghaire which was not very far away. The visibility deteriorated again and real fog began to creep in. This was now serious as we were unsure of our exact position in relation to the dangerous Irish Sea banks where many ships have come to grief. In addition I was concerned that we could get run down by a steamer and although we had a radar reflector, we did not know if we would show up on a ship's radar. We had no V.H.F. and this was before

G.P.S. was thought of so we had a dilemma. We did however have an old B.E.M.E. loop radio direction finder which could help us find our position reasonably accurately if properly tuned in. The battery was low but eventually Harold Brown using all his navigational skills managed to get a reasonable fix on the Kish Light Vessel, although we never saw it. The dilemma was what to do now! Should we try to find the harbour entrance or with the Dunmore East experience still fresh in our minds, should we wait outside until the fog lifted but run the risk of collision. The decision was made for us, as the wind was piping up with a very confused sea when suddenly land appeared out of the fog. We approached the coast cautiously with Kenneth and Winkie's sharp eyes at the bow. We had made our landfall just south of Dunlaoghaire and rolled through the entrance to welcome shelter in the harbour. Well done all hands!

Dunlaoghaire is famous for its hospitality to visiting yachtsman. There are three yacht clubs round the harbour; the Royal Irish, the Royal St. George and the National. Some yachtsmen are foolish enough to try and drink in all of them in the same night as invitations are usually forthcoming from all and the local yachtsmen are always keen to introduce visitors to the joys of Guinness! On anchoring off the Royal Irish Yacht Club it was not long until the club boatman arrived alongside with an invitation for all hands to make use of the club facilities. We all felt a little unsure as we had no go-ashore clothes with us and we did not know if we could go in our sailing gear. We smartened ourselves up as much as possible and the launch came back to take us ashore. We were greeted in the bar by Peter Odlum, a prominent Irish yachtsman who raced his 8 Metre Cruiser Racer *Inismara* on the Clyde and knew us. Showers were provided and he insisted on entertaining us to dinner in the club. The Royal Irish Yacht Club was and still is a wonderful example of a traditional yacht club with silverware, paintings and models. We had a great meal, particularly enjoyed after our on-board cooking efforts and Peter even brought out the club vintage port especially for us.

Winkie left us in Dunlaoghaire and the weather improved which was just as well as we were now down to four. We made a fast passage of 23 hours as far as Lamlash before the wind died and we drifted in icy calm until the next morning. Tom had to get back to work and we rowed him ashore at Rothesay to catch the early steamer. We were now down to three Harold, Kenneth and I, and on arriving at Port Bannatyne we picked up a mooring. It had been a longer passage than anticipated but successful in spite of the weather and a few gear failures. It proved to us how superbly an 8 Metre performs to windward. *Wye* promised to be an exceptional boat and we were looking forward to our first race.

When we brought *Wye* to the Clyde there were already several 8 Metres here. These were *Silja* owned by Dr Weir, *Christina of Cascais* by Kenny Gall and Peter Fairlie, *If,* by Tommy Rose and *Turid II* by George Wolfe. Archie Hardie bought *Severn II* also from Cork and we were soon to be joined by *June* owned by Ian Rose, Tommy's son and *Carron II* by Craig Downie. This made a racing fleet of 8 boats which did not include a few local 8's whose owners were did not race in the class. These were *Margaret, Vagrant II* and *Siris*. The vintage Fife 8 metre *The Truant* was also in Scotland based at Crinan but altered too much to be able to race with us. *Silja* and *Christina* had been racing in the C.C.C. handicap races for a few seasons so they had the advantage of knowing their boats and they were hard to beat at first. *Turid* had sailed to the Clyde from Norway a few years before under Brodie and Malcolm McGregor's ownership who subsequently sold her to George Wolfe. *If* had been one of the Cork boats before Tommy Rose brought her home. This was to be the start of a revival of the largest scratch class to race on the Clyde for many years. It was wonderful to see such a fleet again on the Clyde particularly as most people were interested in I.O.R. rule boats or modern G.R.P. cruisers. I must emphasise that with the exception of Tommy Rose and Dr. Weir, we were all young men and did not have much money to spend on our boats. Most of the yachts had no engines and those had dummy propellers fitted to ensure no advantage over those who had. A local class association was formed to regulate and promote the class which was soon recognised by the Clyde Yacht Clubs Association who provided separate starts for the 8 Metres (the largest yachts of the racing fleet) in all their regattas. This was the first time 8's had raced as a scratch class on the Clyde since the War.

We had an exciting and reasonably successful first season in 1968. In 1969 I became engaged to be married. I had met my fiancé Vivien Lang through sailing as her father owned *Nomad II* a 55 foot ketch rigged motor sailer. Vivien recalls that when they were moored at Fairlie in the *Northward* days, her father would look over to us and say to her and her sister Nicky "Look how the Findlay boys look after their boat - scrubbing decks, polishing brass etc." The Lang girls were much more interested in teenage girls' things such as fashion and magazines than cleaning boats! Kenneth and I knew Vivien and Nicky and often saw then at C.C.C. functions where with their glamorous French mother Martiza, along with their young sister Lydia they made a lasting impression. They were always the "Belles of the Ball" and attracted many admirers. Vivien and I really got to know each other in 1968 at our first West Highland Week in *Wye*. Vivien's father Colin sailed with Tommy Rose on *If* and *Nomad* was a sort of mother ship for the *If* crew. Unlike *Wye, If* had virtually nothing below as Tommy was a keen racing man and did not want any creature comforts. *Wye* on the other hand had basic accommodation with six berths, a cooker and heads and as we usually cruised after the Saturday regattas we had the best of both worlds.

In 1969 we decided to cruise north and Vivien and I, Kenneth and his girlfriend Beth along with my sister Joyce and a platonic friend Jeremy Young made up the crew.

Silja, Christina and Wye at Crinan 1968

We had a great cruise following the Tobermory race which was the subject of an excellent T.V. documentary that year. Magnus Magnussen was the narrator and three yachts had cameramen aboard. We featured briefly when our multi coloured (psychedelic) spinnaker fouled round the forestay (the cameras are always in the wrong place at the wrong time!) but Kenny Gall and his crew in *Christina* were stars along with David Rombach in *Lola*. The third boat featured was Ian Nicholson's *St. Mary* who managed to go aground both in the Kyles and later on the rock at Crinan, all captured on film, it must have been actor's nerves! It was a well produced documentary which really captured the atmosphere and spirit of the race at the end of the wooden boat era. It is a reminder of Clyde yachting in the sixties when boats were much more individual than today and there were many "characters" amongst the owners and crews.

The weather was mixed for our cruise but from Tobermory we sailed over to Coll and across the Minch to the Outer Isles calling at Vatersay and Castlebay in Barra which had hardly changed since our previous visits in *Northward*. We then sailed to Eriskay and walked across the island to Prince Charlie's beach. This is where Charles Edward Stuart landed in Scotland before the 1745 rebellion. At midnight we heard a gale forecast with southerly winds force 8 to 9 and we waited to see what would transpire. At 13.00 the next day the wind was from the south east and blowing straight into the anchorage. It was time to go and we got the anchor aboard. As we had no engine we tacked out of the anchorage under reefed main and small jib. *Wye* took off like a racehorse and we had to be very careful to avoid the submerged rocks. To our sheer delight the yacht's windward performance was shown to its best advantage that day. At the tiller I knew that she would do exactly what I wanted and as we tacked she shot up to windward gaining valuable distance on each tack. Once clear of the entrance we breathed a collective sigh of relief and eased the sheets for Loch Maddy where we hoped to shelter from the gale. The wind increased to force 8 from the south with a big sea running. By this time we had stowed the mainsail and ran on under jib only. We averaged 7 knots over a 4 hour period under jib only and *Wye* handled beautifully like the thoroughbred she is. At 18.30 we entered Loch Maddy and anchored off the pier with 30 fathoms (60 metres approx) of chain down. The gale continued but we were uncomfortable where we were, as if we dragged we would have been driven ashore and of course we had no engine. We set the trysail and storm jib and moved over to a more sheltered anchorage in Ardmaddy bay. Anchored in 2½ fathoms with 25 fathoms of chain and an angel down we all slept like logs.

Onward we sailed to Stornoway with a stop at Loch Ouirn and a visit to the Shiants on the way. This group of islands is uninhabited apart from millions of seabirds and a flock of semi wild sheep. Spectacular cliffs rise from the sea and we sailed between the islands. Suddenly a fierce squall hit us coming directly down from the cliffs. *Wye* was pressed down and we shot dramatically through the gap between two islands to relative calm on the other side. We had a fright and learned the lesson of sailing too close to high cliffs. At anchor at Gravir in Loch Ouirn we heard another poor forecast, this time south westerly 6 to 7. Fierce squalls came down from the hills round us and we left around midday under trysail and working jib. With a lumpy sea from the south and wind around force 6 we eventually reached Stornoway where we anchored at first just inside the lifeboat mooring, moving alongside the fish quay later. We knew Stornoway from our earlier visits and soon we were entertained by Ian Morrison, Charlie's son. He insisted on taking us to the golf club, where although he had never played golf in his life, he was very good on the 19th hole! I proposed to Vivien that evening on the fish quay; hardly the most romantic setting! From Stornoway we returned south via Staffin, Plockton, Kyle of Lochalsh and Mallaig. Most of the time the wind was southerly and we were often reefed but on leaving Mallaig the wind had died and we drifted and sailed gently, eventually arriving at Tobermory. Our time was now up and as we were due to take part in West Highland Week we had to be back at Crinan for the start. Colin Lang in *Nomad* and my parents in their yacht *Romeiro* had seen us as we came through the Dorus Mor and we were welcomed with flares and cheers from the shore. As you can imagine celebrations of our engagement and safe return went on all night.

A few weeks later we celebrated our engagement properly at Tarbert after the C.C.C. Tarbert Race. We had won the race in 1968 but on this occasion, *If* with Michael Rose, Tommy's son and my future brother in law at the helm beat us to the line. My excuse was that my mind was on other things! The party was spectacular with *Wye* tied up alongside *Nomad* and *Romeiro* and other boats. Champagne was flowing all evening and late at night the police warned us not to make so much noise. We all blamed Ian Young as he had the loudest voice but eventually peace reigned. Kenneth and Beth also got engaged a few weeks later and Joyce married John Glen who was a regular *Wye* crew in September. There must have been something about the 8 Metres which brought all this on!

In 1970 an American 8 Metre owner Eugene van Voorhis shipped his yacht *Cheetah* ex *Iskareen* to the Clyde to race with our fleet. This boat had been on the Clyde in the fifties and was designed by Olin Stephens. She was known to be one of the fastest 8 Metres in the world. Eugene also owned *Iroquois* a new boat, also by Olin Stephens and modelled on *Intrepid* the successful America's Cup 12 Metre. This was serious competition and Eugene presented the Royal Northern Yacht Club with a silver trophy for the 8 Metre World Championship to be raced for the first time in 1970 at Rothesay. *Cheetah* was a formidable competitor but did not get things all her own way. She had more and better sails than most of the other boats and although she was definitely faster and stiffer in strong winds the local boats performed well and *Silja* was the first winner of the cup. This trophy is still raced for today and the 8 Metre class has grown over the years.

The World Cup is now an international event held each year in a different country. Sweden, Italy and France have all hosted it and there are plans to come back to the Clyde in 2007. The class has come a long way since our modest efforts in 1968 and there are now several new boats, as well as many restored to their former glory. They now race in three classes. New 8 Metres, Classic 8's and Vintage 8's and in recent years there have been 25 to 30 entries from all over the world. John Lammerts van Bueren from Holland is the class convenor and has with the help of others developed worldwide interest in Metre Boat racing. A reunion dinner was held at the Royal Northern and Clyde Yacht Club in 2000 which was attended by past and present 8 Metre owners and crews from around the world. Olin Stephens who is perhaps the world's most famous yacht designer of his generation was the guest of honour and at 93 years old still healthy and actively sailing. It was fascinating for us to meet all these people and to see videos of recent regattas. We never dreamed that the first World Cup Regatta at Rothesay 30 years before would grow to what it is today. Several famous yachtsmen are involved in International Metre Boat Classes including yacht designers German Frers who owns a vintage 8 and Doug Petersen who has a 10 Metre.

From 1968 to 1973 we had some wonderful racing in *Wye*. We gradually improved in both crewing and helmsmanship and I attribute this to consistency of crew. Although many people sailed with us in *Wye* over the years, we eventually had a hard core who crewed in almost every race. We usually raced with six, sometimes seven or occasionally only five. Although this seems low for the size of boat by modern racing standards, everyone knew their position and job aboard and we soon learned to work as a team. With this practice we began to win races, including the Tobermory and Tarbert races, West Highland Week and Saturday regattas. We had some exciting moments, too many to relate here but I will tell of a few.

On one occasion during Clyde Week my cousin Andrew slipped from the foredeck over the side. We were on a reach and leading at the time, fortunately without a spinnaker set. I was at the helm and immediately gybed and sailed up to the lee of where he was swimming. We hauled him on board and got back to the serious business of the race. Although Andrew received some verbal abuse from certain crew members, all was forgiven when we retrieved our position and won the race.

Another time at a Cove and Kilcreggan Sailing Club regatta one year we were reaching under spinnaker to the finishing line off the clubhouse at Kilcreggan in a close battle with *Turid*. Suddenly a fierce squall hit us and both yachts broached. *Turid's* foredeck hand managed to release the snap shackle and tame the spinnaker. We steadied up, but on crossing the line in first place our multi coloured (psychedelic) spinnaker burst into pieces at exactly the moment the gun went off! It was almost as if it had been loaded with live shot. A spectacular finish indeed! George Findlay (no relation) the Glasgow Herald's yachting correspondent was crewing on *Turid* and there was a photo of the moment when the spinnaker burst in George Findlay was a great character and a free lance journalist for the Herald for many years. He was an Orcadian, had a keen sense of humour and loved sailing and everything to do with it. George usually was invited to race on one of the yachts in most regattas and he had a particular love for the 8 Metres or "Straight Eights" as some people called them to distinguish us from the Cruiser 8's. Some others unkindly referred to us as the "Rentokil Fleet" as our boats were elderly. George's reports were always eagerly awaited on a Monday morning, sometimes we wondered if we were all in the same race!

Wye with her colourful striped spinnaker

George used some colourful language in his articles, spinnakers were "scudding sails" and some "Para Handy" type expressions often appeared. He was an excellent hand and a good seaman and we always enjoyed having him aboard. George was the guest speaker at our annual 8 Metre class dinner on several occasions where he made some very funny speeches.

Most of the eights lost their wooden masts in the first or second season. First *Silja*, then *Christina* and *If,* followed by *Severn* and *June. Turid* lost her wooden mast but also her new aluminium one in the same year. I am sure most were accidental but owners were convinced that metal masts were faster. There was even a special tie for dismasted owners the logo was in the form of a broken spar with the initials E.P.E.G which stood for "ex phallus, ex gratia". We raced for a while with our original spruce mast and I do not think it was a big disadvantage but sadly *June* who had a new Proctor mast broke away from her moorings at Gourock and was totally wrecked. This was an opportunity to buy an almost new aluminium mast which had been salvaged and I negotiated a deal with Ian Rose. The new mast was an improvement, *Wye* was stiffer with the lighter spar and it was easier to tune the rig than before.

The Tobermory race was the big attraction in those days and one year we had our most successful result when we took the lead over the whole fleet at Duart Point picking up a breeze when the rest of the fleet were becalmed. We sailed our solitary way up the Sound of Mull to arrive at Tobermory before the race officers were expecting us. It was early in the day and they were still in the hotel. They had not expected any boat to arrive so quickly. We took our own time and were presented with the Tobermory Bottle – a bottle of Old Mull whisky presented each year to the first boat home. We were not only first home but easily saved our time on handicap. The next 8 Metre arrived about half an hour later. Another year we had a great battle with *Silja* in a close tacking duel up the east side of Calve Island. It was a miracle than neither boat touched the bottom. As someone said - "just go on until you see the whites of the flounders' eyes!" Some of the crew had bets on which boat's crew member would be the first to drink a pint in the Mishnish Hotel in Tobermory. We had nominated my cousin Murray and we arrived in the bay just ahead of *Silja*. Both yachts sailed in very close to the seafront. Murray dived over the side and swam ashore but *Silja* sailed in even closer and their man Douglas Mowat known as the "Black Douglas" followed. Murray got to the Mishnish first but found the public bar door locked. Dripping wet and looking like a wild man with his long hair and beard, he banged on the door which was opened by Willie the unfriendly barman who slammed it in his face with the words "We're no open yet" much to the amusement of a few passers by. Nevertheless we won the bet and the usual festivities ensued. The "Black Douglas" had an unusual party trick of eating glasses. After a few drinks usually late at night, he would simply chew up his glass and swallow the pieces. His skipper Doctor Weir told him that he could do nothing for him if his insides got cut up but undaunted he did this regularly without any ill effects as far as we could see.

Our final year in *Wye,* 1973 provided some of the best racing I have ever experienced. We were competing for the Royal Thames Yacht Club Trophy which had been presented to the class for the best boat over a series of races during the season. It became obvious to us that *Iskareen* (formerly *Cheetah*) which had been sold by Eugene van Voorhis to Eric Maxwell and re-named with her original name was the boat to beat. *Silja* was no longer in the fleet as she had been sold to Finland. During the season we were very evenly matched with *Iskareen*. She was better in a blow and we were faster in light weather and by the final race we both had the same number of firsts. This last race a Royal Clyde Yacht Club event was crucial and the weather was in our favour; a westerly force 3 with sunshine. The start was at Kilcreggan and it was obvious that this would be a close match race between us. We took the lead at first but *Iskareen* was hard on our heels and overhauled us. We changed places several times, in a furious tacking duel and luffing match with the leading boat covering in match racing tradition. On the final run to Gourock from Kirn, we got through *Iskareen's* lee and managed to keep ahead until the finishing line. We finished 11 seconds ahead and claimed the Royal Thames Trophy. The best and most satisfying race any of us had sailed. It is interesting to note that Eric Maxwell and James Howden Hume both from the Clyde are as far as I know the only two people in the world ever to own a 12 Metre, 8 Metre and 6 Metre all at the same time. Eric Maxwell owned *Sceptre, Isakareen* and *Gosling* in 1971 and James Howden Hume had *Trivia, Froya* and *Johan* in 1946.

This was alas the end of the Clyde 8 Metre class. This was said before in the 1950's and the class was surprisingly revived. Perhaps it will happen again as internationally the class has never been stronger. *Wye* was bought by Siggi Svensen from Stockholm and he owned her from 1973 until 2003 when she went to France. *If* has been restored and is now owned by Peter Wilson of Aldeburgh Boat Yard in Sussex. *Siris* now also in England was completely re-built by Fairlie Restorations of Hamble. The other members of the Clyde fleet are all as far as I know in good condition in different countries - *Christina* (now *Ilderim*) in Belgium, *Silja* in Finland, *Carron II* in Norway, *Severn* in Canada and *Turid* in Switzerland. It is wonderful to see the class in such good heart and we look forward to seeing them again at the forthcoming World Cup on the Clyde. This will be the first time the 8's have raced here for over 30 years and will perhaps be the largest fleet of 8 Metres ever to race on the Clyde as perhaps up to 40 boats could enter.

Kenneth and I reluctantly decided to sell *Wye* as the class was breaking up and more importantly we were now both married with babies and a racing 8 Metre is not the best boat in which to bring up children. Our wives were relieved when we decided to buy a more modern and comfortable vessel. This was *Muchacha,* a new 39 Foot One Ton Cup class boat from Argentina. German Frers the designer had trained with Sparkman and Stephens in New York before returning to Buenos Aires to his family boat building business. The Frers 39 was designed to measure as a One Tonner but was not as extreme as some of the class. Relatively heavy compared to others, she was an excellent cruiser-racer and we learned a lot about modern yacht design and sailing techniques in her. We took part in the first of the now popular Scottish Series events; then called the "Comet Wheel" later the "Tomatin Trophy" followed by other sponsors over the years. This first regatta was held at Tobermory and finished in Skye. Nowadays the whole regatta is held at Tarbert Loch Fyne. Our children had their first experiences of cruising on *Muchacha* but after a couple of years Kenneth and I decided to go our separate ways and give up serious racing at least for a while. I bought *Skulmartin* a Hustler 30 designed by Kim Holman and Kenneth bought *Tinkatoo* a "Rummer" yawl also by Holman. This was a temporary situation for me and I was soon taken with a new design from Sweden which Bill McKay and Ian Scott Watson were marketing at Troon. I had a trial sail with Bill on a breezy autumn day when he told me of his experiences sailing the boat over from Sweden.

This new boat, a Fiskatra S30 had many attractive features which appealed to me. Firstly she was a metre boat of sorts. The design was based on the 30 Square Metre Class and secondly she had good accommodation unlike the original racing 30 Squares. I ordered a new boat and *Flicka* was delivered to Troon in the spring of the following year. At 41 feet overall, 30 feet on the waterline with 8 feet beam and light displacement, *Flicka* certainly had metre boat characteristics. She was fast and easily handled and from the family cruising perspective she had six berths in three cabins – fore cabin, main saloon and an after cabin with sitting headroom which was ideal for the children. As kids often get bored when sailing we would allow them to stay up late and sleep when underway during the day. In the after cabin we were always sure where they were at all times, as they had to squeeze past the helmsman to get out. Unfortunately my girls did not take well to sailing and after a disastrous holiday in 1985 when the weather was atrocious we decided to put her on the market. 1985 was the year of the C.C.C. 75th anniversary celebrations and we took part in the passage through the canal and the muster at Crinan and Tobermory. Unfortunately Vivien was not very well so we sailed back after the "Sunflower" raft up at Loch Drumbuie where the world record for a large number of yachts tied up in a circle was set. One other incident comes to mind. On passage from Tobermory to Canna another year in a strong south-westerly with a lumpy sea Vivien and the children were below as Jim King and I sailed the boat. On deck we were blissfully unaware that the dreaded seasickness was taking its toll and suddenly there was a loud shriek from Vivien as the toilet seat flew out of the hatch just missing my right ear! The loo seat had fallen on my daughter Suzanne's head and in her anger and frustration she ripped it off and hurled it out the hatch.

Chapter 5 - "Doon the Watter"

Having been born in Glasgow and known the river Clyde all my life I have always had an interest and love for Scotland's largest and perhaps most interesting river. Although not one of the world's great rivers such as the Amazon or Nile, the Clyde enjoys worldwide fame for shipbuilding over 300 years which made "Clydebuilt" a byword for quality in maritime circles.

Before speaking of shipbuilding we will start at the source of the river near Elvanfoot in Lanarkshire, where several insignificant streams merge to form a larger one which meanders down the Clyde Valley, over the Falls of Clyde to Hamilton where in recent times the river was diverted to form the artificial Strathclyde Loch. The Clyde then flows through Glasgow and down the Clyde Estuary, also known as the Firth of Clyde and finally to the sea. As in the lyrics of the popular song:-

> *I dream of a river I'm happy beside*
> *The song that I sing is the song of the Clyde*
> *Of all Scottish rivers it's dearest to me*
> *It flows from Leadhills all the way to the sea.*

At one time the Clyde was very shallow all the way through Glasgow down to Port Glasgow which was the original port for the area, as ships could not proceed up the river. It was also a great salmon river and although the salmon disappeared in the 20th century due to pollution from the shipyards some have now come back since the river has been cleaned up. Although nothing like the days when a local by law prohibited employers from giving their employees salmon more than three times a week, anglers now catch fish in the upper reaches from time to time. I had an unusual experience a few years ago when at the riverside opposite the Glasgow Sheriff Court building in the city centre, I saw a seal swimming in the river. This would have been unthinkable a few years before. The seal had either badly lost its way, or it had found something to eat in the river!

It would seem unlikely that such a shallow river could float some of the world's largest and most famous ships but the saying "Glasgow made the Clyde and the Clyde made Glasgow" has more than a grain of truth to it. In the 17th century Scottish merchants began to develop trade for herring, textiles and salt with America and Europe importing for example tobacco, cotton, sugar and rum from America and wine, brandy and other luxuries from France and imports from other European countries. Limited attempts were made to dredge the river and in 1786 a survey showed that the depth at Bowling was only two feet at low water. An ingenious scheme was begun in 1770 by John Golborne to deepen the Clyde and 117 jetties and banks were constructed along the banks to force the tidal stream into the centre of the river thus causing it to scour and deepen all the way from the centre of Glasgow to Greenock. This was a remarkable feat of civil engineering and it is hard to understand exactly how this was achieved with the primitive equipment of the time but indeed Glasgow made the Clyde. Eventually steam dredgers were invented and today there is as depth of at least 25 feet in the channel which is still dredged by Clydeport.

After the Act of Union in 1707 Glasgow became the major European centre for importing tobacco from America. Until the War of Independence (1779-1783), most of the ships used for this trade were built in America as there was a plentiful supply of timber there. The war caused ship owners to buy elsewhere and this lead to a new and flourishing shipbuilding industry being established primarily on the lower Clyde at Greenock, Port Glasgow and Dumbarton. John Scott formed his company at Greenock in 1711 which was still building ships until recent times. In 1769 James Watt of Greenock developed his steam engine and built the first commercially viable steamship, the *Comet* in 1812. An exact replica can be seen today outside Port Glasgow town hall, very close to where the original vessel was built. Although steam was the propulsion of the future, large numbers of sailing vessels were built in the 1800's. Many famous ships including the tea clippers *Cutty Sark, Ariel* and *Taiping,* the *Pass of Balmaha* which became notorious in World War I as the *See Adler* a German decoy ship. The cargo carrying 4 mast barques *Archibald Russell, Olivebank* and *Moshulu* and many, many others were all built on the Clyde. There are only five Clydebuilt sailing ships left afloat in the world today. These are the *Glenlee* which is moored in Glasgow, the *Falls of Clyde* in Honolulu, the *Balclutha* in San Franciso, the *Pommern* in Mariehamn, Finland and the *Moshulu* in Philadelphia. None of these vessels go to sea now but all have been restored and can be visited.

As time went on steam replaced sail and the Clyde yards built substantial numbers of vessels. In 1841 Robert Napier who made a major impact on shipbuilding opened a yard in Govan to produce iron steamers. This yard is generally acknowledged to be the start of modern shipbuilding on the Clyde. Clydeside engineers were considered to be the best in the world both in the yards and at sea and it was said that if you shouted "Jock" down the engine room hatch in any ship a Glasgow voice would reply "Aye". World famous passenger liners were built at John Brown's yard at Clydebank. The *Queen Mary, Queen Elizabeth* and *QE2* and in the early years of the century the *Lusitania* and *Aquitania,* the first vessels to exceed 30,000 tons were also built there. Many ships of all types and sizes were constructed on the Clyde during the 20th century. Merchant ships, passenger liners, warships including battleships, cruisers, destroyers and frigates, ferries and large yachts all made their way down the Clyde slipways. In 1960 there were still 30 shipyards on the river between Glasgow and Ardrossan. *Fairfield, Harland and Wolff, Connell, Barclay Curle, Yarrow, Alexander Stephen, Scott, Lithgow and Denny* are all gone now but were once renowned. Today only two yards remain in Glasgow and one in Port Glasgow. It is a tragedy that at a time when many new luxury cruise ships are in commission and the new *Queen Mary II*, the world's largest passenger liner recently completed in France that the Clyde has completely lost the ability to build such vessels. The vast majority of world trade is still carried by ships but unfortunately recession in the 1950's, management and union disputes and subsidised competition from abroad eventually dealt a death blow to the Clyde. Where we once dominated the industry there remains only a shadow of former glories. Skills once passed down from father to son almost completely disappeared in a few decades. I like statistics and it may be on interest to note that it is said that at its peak the Clyde produced over 25% of the world's merchant ships. During World War II the Clyde yards built almost 2,000 ships including the famous "Mulberry Harbour"- so essential for the invasion of Normandy, converted over 600 and repaired more than 25,000. The Clyde's contribution to the war effort was invaluable and incalculable.

QE2 at John Browns with the Sir Winston Churchill

In its heyday the Clyde in Glasgow was a busy river. Queen's and Princes docks and the riverside berths were all full of ships right up to the first bridge at the Broomielaw. The "Cluthas" were small river boats which plied the upper reaches. The passenger ferries and later vehicle ferries provided crossings at various places in Glasgow, Renfrew and Erskine and the general traffic of coasters, barges, tugs and river steamers all worked on the river. The Clyde passenger steamers were an essential part of the Glasgow population's summer holidays. At the "Glasgow Fair" weekend in July every year the working population made a mass exodus to the coast, "Doon the Watter" as the expression goes. Seaside towns such as Dunoon, Rothesay, Largs and Millport were packed with holidaymakers and there was a large fleet of over forty handsome, fast paddle and turbine steamers to take the traffic. It was not only at the "Fair" that the steamers were busy but most of the time, as this was the main method of communication between the coastal communities in those years. There were over 80 piers around the coast for passengers from Craigendoran at Helensburgh across to Greenock and Gourock, from Kilcreggan to Hunter's Quay and Kirn to Dunoon and up all the sea lochs. It was easier to travel by fast steamer in the 1930's than by road or car ferry today. Many well-off families rented or owned houses on the coast for the summer months and businessmen travelled by steamer and train to their work in Glasgow returning in the evenings. The Clyde steamers were famous and names from the past include the *Columba* which could steam at 21 knots and the *Queen Alexandra* which could make 24 knots. The *Talisman, Duchess of Montrose, Duchess of Hamilton, Caledonia, Jupiter, Lucy Ashton* and *Jeannie Deans* were all still sailing when I was a boy and the *Queen Mary* was built in 1933 before the Cunard liner of the same name. As a mark of respect the owners changed her name to *Queen Mary II* to allow the Cunarder to take the name. The *Queen Mary II* is now in London berthed in the Thames as a floating restaurant.

The sole surviving Clyde steamer in commission is the *Waverley*, "The last seagoing paddle steamer in the world" as the company's advertising states. The *Waverley* was built in 1947 by Inglis yard at Pointhouse in Glasgow and took part in the D day evacuation in France during the war. Thanks to the Paddle Steamer Preservation Society the ship has been restored and is in immaculate condition. It is a great pleasure to sail in her down the Clyde or through the Kyles of Bute and to experience the feel, sounds and smells of a real steamship. The engine room is open to view and the huge pistons and paddle wheels hold passengers in rapt attention for hours. The *Waverley* has a very busy summer season and travels as far south as the Solent each year where she stays for a few weeks giving our English cousins a "Clyde Steamer Experience".

Imagine now a trip down the Clyde on the *Waverley* from her berth in Glasgow. We first pass through Bell's Bridge which has been opened for us. We wave to the barque *Glenlee* at her berth and proceed downstream where many new and expensive riverside flats stand where ships were once built and docked. At Clydebank on the starboard side, it is still possible to see the remains of the slipways of John Brown's where the "Queens" were built. The slipways are angled to allow large ships to launch across the river into the mouth of the river Cart, as the Clyde was too narrow for such large vessels. I remember watching the launch in 1968 of the last liner to be built for Cunard on the Clyde - the *Queen Elizabeth 2* or *QE2* as she is also known. A huge crowd saw her gigantic hull slowly slide down the ways, gathering speed across the river into the mouth of the Cart. It was a nostalgic moment and we all knew that this was the last of an era. Unfortunately Clydebank like most of the rest of the riverfront is devoid of any shipbuilding today and derelict land and abandoned sheds still litter the riverside in many places where new property has still to be built.

We now sail under the Erskine Bridge and approach the village of Bowling. Scott & Sons once had their yard here but it is now long gone. One interesting new development is the re-opening of the Forth and Clyde Canal. The canal had been virtually derelict since the sixties but it is once again possible to sail from the Clyde to the Forth. Thanks to the new Falkirk Wheel boat lift, boats can now link up to the Union Canal in the east. The British Waterways Board have made a huge investment in all the Scottish canals and boating enthusiasts can now enjoy the revived Forth and Clyde Canal again. With the Kirkpatrick hills to starboard and the low Renfrewshire hills to port, we gradually leave industrial Clydeside. Dumbarton is next with its spectacular 240 foot high basalt rock. The castle on top of the rock once imprisoned the Scottish patriot William Wallace in 1305. Although Dumbarton was an engineering and shipbuilding town where Denny's yard once flourished most of this industry has gone now. The famous tea clipper the *Cutty Sark* was built here and the yacht yard of R. McAllister now Sandpoint Marina, no longer builds yachts but provides good winter storage facilities. The river meanders down towards the sea passing Helensburgh where John Logie Baird the inventor of television lived. On the opposite bank of the river which is much broader here lies Port Glasgow. It is noticeable that as the river widens the dredged channel remains the same width all the way down to the Tail of the Bank where the Firth begins. It is a somewhat unnerving to be sailing down the narrow channel in a small boat and being overtaken by a huge ship with little space between.

Port Glasgow first prospered before the Clyde was deepened but after that time along with its neighbour Greenock became a major shipbuilding and engineering centre. Both towns became famous for the large number of sailing ships built in its yards during the 19th Century. Russell's yard for example built 20 ships a year for years on end. The *Glenlee* mentioned earlier was built by Rodger's yard in 1896. Rope, canvas and all the various materials and parts necessary for a ship were made here or in the Glasgow area. In more recent times Hastie's engineering works and other firms made most of the heavy mechanical items for large vessels, engines, steering gear, boilers etc. Today the sole remaining Lower Clyde yard of Ferguson's still builds ferries and other small vessels for the U.K. and overseas. Fergusons is the only family owned shipbuilder on the Clyde and it is a pleasure to see a vessel on the stocks or at the fitting out berth. The large Greenock dry dock and Garvel dry dock and repair yard are also still in business but much of the land formerly used for shipbuilding now contains offices and flats. Engineering in the form of electronics replaced shipbuilding, as IBM has a large computer plant at Spango Valley in Greenock, although even this is changing now. Greenock was also famous for sugar, as raw sugar cane was imported and refined in the town. Gourock lies next to Greenock and is more of a residential town with attractive villas facing the sea and the white painted Royal Gourock Yacht Club on the seafront. The building was presented to the club by Major James Coats of the Coats thread family in Paisley and it looks out to what some call the finest view in the world. From the balcony one can look across to the Cowal shore and the Holy Loch, Kilcreggan and Loch Long. In the distance we see Helensburgh and the Gareloch with the mountains beyond, sometimes snow topped in winter and early spring. The Royal Gourock has always been a racing club and many regattas have been held from the starting line off the clubhouse. Evening racing for the Loch Long and Piper dayboat classes as well as handicap racing take place every week in the summer and many yachts are moored off the club in spite of the competition nowadays from nearby marinas.

Before leaving the Upper Firth we must explore the sea lochs; the Gareloch, Loch Long and the Holy Loch. Each of these three lochs (or Fiords) has its unique characteristics. The Gareloch is a pretty homely sort of place with low surrounding hills rising above substantial houses on the east side at Rhu and Shandon. The imposing clubhouse of the Royal Northern and Clyde Yacht Club stands in its leafy grounds at Rhu. The Royal Northern Yacht Club merged with the Royal Clyde Yacht Club in 1978, four years after celebrating its 150th anniversary. The Royal Northern was founded in 1824 and the Royal Clyde in 1856. The Royal Clyde formerly occupied a substantial building at Hunter's Quay near the Holy Loch. The R.N.C.Y.C building is a large Victorian villa containing paintings, photographs and models illustrating Clyde yachting history over 180 years. The club was once involved in the America's Cup when in 1887 the G. L. Watson designed *Thistle* unsuccessfully challenged the Burgess designed *Volunteer*. In 1947 the club received a challenge from the U.S.A. for the Seawanhaka Cup in the 6 Metre class. Another *Thistle* designed by David Boyd was commisioned by Ronald Teacher. Unfortunately a different boat *Johan* owned by James Douglas Hume was selected but defeated. Many other international racing events in 8 Metres, 6 Metres, Solings, Etchells 22 and International One Design classes have been hosted by the club which is the second oldest in the British Isles. On the west shore of the Gareloch is the site of the former McGruer's yard which I describe in chapter 7. Alas, houses now stand where many famous yachts once were born but Silver's yard at Rosneath and the former Admiralty sheds, once occupied by McGruers are still in business. The Gareloch is the home of many yachts and there are moorings around the coast particularly at Rhu where Rhu Marina provides secure berthing at the entrance to the loch. At Faslane near the head of the loch is the heavily guarded Clyde Submarine Base. Any boat sailing up the loch is soon chased away if it ventures too close. The description of Faslane bay taken from the Clyde Cruising Club sailing directions of 1932 recommends Faslane as an anchorage and suggests yachts "anchor in 3 to 5 fathoms anywhere in the bay", an impossible feat today!

The next loch is Loch Long. Between the Gareloch and Loch Long lies the village of Kilcreggan directly opposite Gourock. Kilcreggan boasts a pleasant collection of Victorian villas rising up the hill with the small boatyard of McGrouther's to the east of the pier. The McGrouther brothers have run this yard for many years and an astonishing variety of classic boats lay up there in the winter. Perhaps the most interesting yacht here is the Clyde 17/19 foot class Fife designed *Hattasoo*. Built in 1894 she soon outclassed the other boats in the class. 17/19 refers to the size – 17 feet on the waterline, 19 feet overall and it is a tribute to her designer and builder William Fife as well as to the McGrouther brothers that she is not only in excellent condition but can still win races today. She took first prize in the small boat class at the Fife regatta in 2003. Off Kilcreggan lies the "Minister's Rock" This is an unmarked rock and many racing yachts have either bumped against it or stuck on it at some time. Yours truly is no exception. A few years ago I was sailing with a friend one evening off

Kilcreggan in my small gaff sloop *Ruach*. It was a beautiful warm summer night with a light breeze. We were looking at the shore and admiring the view; quite oblivious to the rock which I confess I had almost forgotten of, when suddenly we stopped with a large bump. Looking over the side we could clearly see we were exactly on top of the rock and the tide was falling. My gallant crew member stripped to his underclothes and as I leaned out on the boom as far as possible to heel the boat over, he jumped overboard into only three feet of water and pushed us off before the tide could hold us. He certainly deserved his pint in the club that night and I now know exactly where the rock is.

"Loch Long is very fine and Loch Fyne is very long" is a well known saying. Loch Long is the longest sea loch in the Upper Firth. 15 miles from Cove to the head, the loch is surrounded by high mountains and at the head Ben Arthur known as the "Cobbler" towers above the village of Arrocher. Loch Long could be described by some to be a gloomy place and few yachts venture far up the loch. This is partly due to the Naval Base at Coulport where boats are discouraged from sailing too close. On the west side the smaller Loch Goil is more often visited. This is a pleasant loch and has altogether a more friendly feeling than the upper reaches of Loch Long. Next along the coast is the Holy Loch, the smallest of the Clyde lochs. The hamlets of Strone and Kilmun are situated between the two lochs. It is a fact that if you look seaward from Strone Point, the first land one would reach if sailing on a straight course is Teneriffe as a straight line would miss the Isle of Man, Ireland and Cornwall. At one time the two yacht building yards of Alexander Robertson and Morris and Lorimer turned out racing and cruising yachts by several designers. Robertson's David Boyd designed many racing yachts including the 12 Metre America's Cup challengers Sceptre and Sovereign. Both yards closed some time ago and the loch was the home of the American Polaris submarine fleet for several years. The U.S. Navy has left now and the Holy Loch has returned to its previous tranquillity with a small marina now on the site of the former Morris and Lorimer's yard. At the entrance to the Holy Loch lies Hunter's Quay where the Royal Clyde Yacht Club had its clubhouse from 1872 until it became a hotel in the sixties. The Clyde Fortnight was the highlight of the racing season in the past and in the end of the 19th and early years of the 20th century huge racing yachts such as the *Britannia, Santanita, Vigilant, Valkyrie and Shamrock* battled for trophies. In 1885 a spectacular and tragic collision with loss of life between *Santanita* and *Valkyrie* led to changes in the racing rules concerning professional helmsmen. The mast of one of these yachts stood as the club flagpole for many years. Next to Hunter's Quay is the village of Kirn and next again the town of Dunoon a holiday resort famed for the "Cowal Gathering" the highland games held every year in August which is one of the largest gatherings in Scotland.

Sailing down Firth we pass the Cloch lighthouse to port and along the coast to Inverkip where Kip Marina was created from the excavation of gravel from the mouth of the river Kip. This is home to several hundred yachts and along with the marinas at Largs, Troon and Ardrossan, has changed yachting habits on the Clyde for ever. Most boats are berthed in marinas today and as this is more secure and safe than lying to moorings, particularly in the autumn and winter months, the number of yachts berthed on the Clyde has grown substantially in my lifetime. Many boats are in commission all the year round and most clubs have "Frostbite" winter racing events. A few miles south of Kip lies Largs, another seaside holiday town with a substantial retired elderly population. Although there is no natural harbour at Largs, Largs Yacht Haven was created 25 years ago by the construction of substantial stone breakwaters providing almost 700 berths. Largs is one of the best locations on the Clyde for the cruising yachtsman. Being close to Bute and only 15 miles from Arran, Largs channel is sheltered by the island of Great Cumbrae with the town of Millport at its south end. There is a shuttle car ferry service to the Great Cumbrae with a bus connection to Millport. The island is only about 4 miles long and many visitors hire bicycles to ride round the island which is a pleasant afternoon's activity. Millport boasts the smallest cathedral in Britain, the Episcopal "Cathedral of the Isles" which is a delightful church building situated in leafy surroundings back from the seafront.

The village of Fairlie next to Largs was at one time the home of three generations of William Fife. The first William Fife started building boats at Fairlie around 1803 where he rented land from the Earl of Glasgow for the princely sum of one shilling per annum (5p). Once the business grew this was increased to £1! The yard built small boats and skiffs and in 1812 his first real yacht the *Lamlash* of 50 tons was completed. Her owner James Hamilton became the first admiral of the Royal Northern Yacht Club. Yachting had not properly developed as a sport until 15 to 20 years after the yard was formed but following the success of Henry Bell's *Comet* the first steamship, William Fife was persuaded to build the *Industry* a similar 66 foot vessel. This remarkable ship was the first to have geared paddle wheels in a paddle box and was nicknamed the "Coffee Grinder" due to the noise she made when underway. The *Industry* was the first cargo carrying steamship and was so well built that she worked for 55 years. She was eventually broken up in 1882 and her engine can still be seen today in the Glasgow Museum of Transport.

Although Fife could have become a wealthy man by building steamers his sole ambition was to build boats that were "fast and bonnie". Orders for yachts were few at that time but Fife built many fast fishing smacks and trading vessels before yacht building eventually became the yard's main activity. Yacht design was further developed by his son William Fife II born in 1821 followed by his son the third William Fife who was to take the Fife reputation all round the world. There were over 800 yachts build at Fairlie over the generations and when one considers the location of the yard it seems miraculous that large yachts could be built and launched into the shallow water of the bay. A floating dock was the ingenious answer which allowed even vessels as large as the 105 foot 260 ton yacht *Shamrock* with a draught of over 10 feet to be built and launched at Fairlie. Although Fairlie has such important associations with yachting there is almost nothing left to show of it today. Fife's yard has been sold and built over with houses. William Fife III had no family and his was the last generation. The sole remaining sign of Fife at Fairlie is the weathervane on the steeple of the church which is a bronze replica of the yawl *Latifa*. *Latifa* along with many other Fife yachts survives today and was restored at McGruer's yard. Fife yachts are much sought after by wealthy owners and have become very valuable. I write more on Fife and his yachts in chapter 7.

On the other side of the Firth lies the Isle of Bute. This attractive island has much to offer from the sands of Kilchattan and Ettrick bays to the beauty of the Kyles of Bute and the contrasting grandeur of "Mount Stuart" home of the Marquis of Bute. Rothesay is the only town on the island and in their heyday Clyde steamers raced to be the first to the pier to uplift their passengers. Travel to the mainland is now by Calmac ferry from Wemyss Bay or via the small ferry at Rhubodach in the Kyles at Colintraive. The Kyles of Bute is one of the most delightful cruising areas in the Clyde and some people do not always appreciate what we have on our doorstep only a short distance from Glasgow. In my view there is no comparison with other famous yachting centres such as the Solent or English East Coast which are hopelessly overcrowded today. Navigating the Kyles we sail through the narrows at the "Burnt Islands" so named as legend has it that the defeated army of King Haakon of Norway cremated the bodies of the dead Vikings there after the battle of Largs in 1263. This battle won by King Alexander III of Scotland finally brought the 450 year Norse rule of Scotland to an end.

Once through the narrows Tignabruaich lies to starboard beside the neighbouring villages of Kames and Auchenlochan. On the Bute side the scenery is decorated with the "Maids of Bute", painted stones resembling two girls in coloured dresses, immortalised in Neil Munro's "Para Handy Tales". As we leave the Kyles we round Ardlamont Point sometimes cruelly described as "the Clyde yachtsman's Cape Horn". This is the entrance to Loch Fyne which is the longest loch in the Clyde, some 35 miles to the head. East Loch Tarbert is a popular and safe harbour and Ardrishaig further north is the eastern end of the Crinan Canal. Inverary lies near the head of the loch on the east side but due to the long sail up the loch is not as often frequented by yachts. Tarbert is a wonderful natural harbour and the most Hebridean of the Clyde anchorages separated from the west coast of Kintyre by only a mile. It is here that the Norseman Magnus Barefoot dragged his galley overland. This was as a result of a treaty between Magnus and King Malcolm III in 1093 granting him possession of all islands which his galleys could pass around. Seated aboard a galley, he had his men haul it across the land on rollers thus laying claim to most of Kintyre.

Tarbert's main activity is fishing and at one time the boats were so numerous that one could walk from one side of the harbour to the other on their decks. This was in the days of the plentiful Loch Fyne herring and the local skiffs were developed for this and other forms of fishing. The ruined castle overlooking the harbour was built by Robert the Bruce in 1325 and on one occasion James IV summoned his parliament there. Dickie's yard is sadly no more but once produced large numbers of fishing boats and many yachts. Peter Dickie served his apprenticeship under William Fife and returned to Tarbert to design and build some very successful cruising yachts including my old yacht *Macaria*.

Finally we will have a look at Arran on our short cruise. Often called "Scotland in Miniature" the island is about 17 miles long and has only two sheltered anchorages - Lamlash on the east side and Loch Ranza on the North. Brodick is also popular for yachts but it is inadvisable to lie there overnight if the wind has any easterly in it, as the bay is quite open to that direction. Arran has been a popular holiday destination for many generations of Glasgow families and some have settled there in their retirement. The highest peak "Goat Fell" at 2,866 feet is climbed by many visitors and Brodick castle, ancestral home of the Duke of Montrose with its beautiful gardens is worth a visit. Parts of the castle date from the 13th century and are associated with Robert the Bruce as it was here he awaited the signal that his followers were ready to rally round him. Sailors tend to see only the coastal places but Arran has much to offer those who are willing to walk or drive inland. A trip across the island soon confirms the "Scotland in Miniature" description. Mountain and glen, moor and forest, croft and farm, all are there with abundant wildlife. I remember one year when we were racing in our 8 Metre yacht *Wye* when we had to take shelter from a southerly gale and anchored off Catacol Bay on the west side. This was the one and only time I anchored off the west coast of Arran.

Ailsa Craig or "Paddy's Milestone" is a basalt rock of 1,114 feet at the entrance to the Firth. A spectacular sight the rock has been a landmark for seamen since time immemorial. Many people have seen Ailsa Craig on T.V. as a backdrop to golf championships at Troon but it also has worldwide fame as the place where curling stones come from. More accurately where the special granite from which curling stones are made was quarried. The quarry is closed now and the lighthouse is automated so no-one lives there any more. Visitors are few and far between but yachts occasionally anchor in good weather and soon find that Ailsa Craig is a haven for birdwatchers. Thousands of gulls, gannets and other seabirds fill the air with their cries and the rocks are white from their droppings.

And so we leave the Clyde. I have only touched on a few places. There are many more stories one could tell but I just want to give you a taste. Some of you may know the Clyde well, others may have known it in the past and more have only heard of it. I hope this brief description will encourage you to come and see our river for yourself. There is plenty of room, bring your boat if you have one or charter, you will be made very welcome.

Chapter 6 - "Tir nan og"

Cruising has been my main interest over the years and "Tir nan og" (land of the ever young) is the Gaelic name given to the western seaboard of Scotland. Described by many including the late Eric Hiscock as the finest cruising ground in the world, we Scots sometimes take it for granted. Everyone knows the weather can be truly awful and visitors soon discover our midges, (or the midges discover the visitors!) but somehow the good days; and there are many more than some people would admit to, make up for the gales and rain which even in summer are frequent. I am not going to try and write a pilot book or even less a tourist guide, there are many such publications available, but simply recall events and people in some of my favourite places.

There is a special atmosphere and light on the west coast and the western isles in particular. When the sun shines there is a certain luminosity about the scenery which many artists have tried to capture on paper or canvas. The view of the "Small Isles" Rhum, Eigg and Muck from the mainland at sunset on a fine evening is something which touches the senses in a special way. The broad sweep of pure white sand on a Hebridean beach with crystal clear water where one can see the bottom in over 5 fathoms, or the mysterious dark grandeur of a sea loch where the hills come down to the depths below, are all unique. The best way to see these parts is from the deck of a small boat. Of course you don't have to be in a yacht to experience the west coast, but in your own boat you can really explore and go where you please, subject only to the wind and tides.

The West Coast of Scotland has an irregular coastline of some 1,400 miles indented with many sea lochs and around 600 islands. The scenery changes dramatically from the Cuillin mountains of Skye to the flat landscape of Tiree; from the basalt rocks of Staffa to the white sands of Barra. There is an infinite variety of views of hill and island, mountain and loch proving the exploring yachtsman with a choice of anchorage and harbours found in few other places. One is always conscious of history in these parts and Scotland has a turbulent and violent past. The west suffered severely from the effects of the infamous Highland Clearances, when many people were forcibly removed from their crofts and replaced with sheep by the landowners in the nineteenth century. This caused serious depopulation of many islands and mainland communities which have never recovered. As a result many parts of the west are very thinly populated.

Mull from Kerrera

Sailing in Scottish waters should be considered with care by inexperienced yachtsman and all should prepare for the conditions. The weather can change very quickly and the coastline is exposed to the Atlantic in many places. Tides can also be tricky, and the need to anchor in remote anchorages requires the correct ground tackle and knowledge of how to use it. The Clyde Cruising Club has published their excellent sailing directions for almost 100 years. This invaluable pilot book was compiled by club members and is regularly updated. It consists of information about virtually every harbour and anchorage along with sketch charts and local knowledge. Every yacht cruising in Scotland should have a copy aboard.

Every summer from an early age our family holidays were spent cruising in Scotland. We explored many places in our different family boats.

I have many memories of that time, some have already been described in previous chapters but I would like to tell you a little of the geography and history of this part of Scotland. If you are not already familiar with it, I hope you will understand its fascination. The Western Isles really start in the Firth of Clyde with the islands of Arran, Bute and the Cumbraes a short distance from Glasgow. The Clyde has been the centre of Scottish sailing since yachts first sailed in these waters but for me the Western Isles really start at Crinan. There is something special about being in the sea lock, waiting for the brown water to go down, hearing the lock gates creaking open and seeing the first glimpse of the Dorus Mor and the islands of Scarba and Jura beyond. It seems as if a door to a magic world has just opened and no matter how many years you have made the passage through the canal from Ardrishaig to Crinan, it is always with a wonderful sense of anticipation that you stand on deck waiting for that moment. Crinan is a special place. The village if you can call it that; consists of a few houses, the boatyard and at the centre overlooking the canal basin, the Crinan Hotel. Run by Nick Ryan and his artist wife Francis McDonald, they have seen many yachts come and go over the years and sailors from many parts have visited the hotel. Nick is a yachtsman and owned *Scarbh* a similar boat to my father's *Tunnag* for many years.

The Crinan canal was first opened in 1801 and Queen Victoria sailed along it in 1847 in a specially built Royal Barge. The canal was originally used by commercial and fishing vessels saving them the often dangerous 80 mile passage round the Mull of Kintyre. The famous Clyde "Puffers" were built to fit the Crinan Canal locks. These were small flat bottomed iron steam vessels which evolved from the sailing gabbarts, ketches and schooners. The puffer became well known to the general public through the tales of "Para Handy" by Neil Munro in the early 1900's and they have been part of Scottish folklore ever since. Neil Munro was a friend of Colin McPhail's father. Colin was a good friend and sailing companion of my father and sailed as one of the crew in *Eileen*. Colin and his father before him were ship owners and owned several puffers until the late sixties. They were all named after Scottish glens; *Genshira, Glen Cloy, Glen Rosa* etc. The McPhail family hailed from Inverary in Argyll and many of the Para Handy stories are set in Kintyre. Neil Munro also named the bad tempered engineer of Para Handy's *Vital Spark* Dan McPhail as a joke on his friend.

I remember the puffers when they still used the canal. They carried coal, building materials and almost everything else to the islands. As they could be beached and dry out at low water, they could go almost anywhere, not being dependent on piers or harbours. Unfortunately times changed and the ubiquitous and much loved puffer was no longer economic. A few survive, two of the Vic class which were built in World War 2 as fleet service vessels when the admiralty considered their design to be the most suitable for the purpose. *Vic 32* carries charter passengers on west coast cruises and *Auld Reekie* which was re-named *Vital Spark* for a BBC series of the Para Handy stories has been laid up for several years with an uncertain future. There is also the *Spartan* a diesel puffer owned by the Scottish Maritime Museum at Irvine which has been recently restored. There have been a few attempts to carry on the puffer trade. The *Eilean Easdale* worked under private ownership for a while but could not make a living. Freight is carried almost exclusively by road transport nowadays and Caledonian McBrayne's vehicle ferries cover all the major islands.

Fishing boats were also regular canal users. Clyde based boats often worked north of Crinan for clams (scallops) and lobsters amongst other catches, and the shortcut through the canal was convenient particularly in the winter months. A fleet of fishing boats is still berthed in Crinan basin where they return to unload their catches on the quayside. Due to the decline of the Scottish fishing industry few boats go through the canal now, which brings us to the main source of income for the British Waterways Board – the yachts. Yachtsmen have used the canal since its early days but as the sport has grown in popularity many prefer to spend a couple of days in its calm leafy stretches than battle with wind and tides off the Mull. At peak times such as West Highland week or the Tobermory race, the canal is really busy and queues can form to get through. In *Wye* we had to rely on getting a tow from other yachts as we had no engine. *If, Severn* and *June* were also engineless, and much fun was had in getting all the eights through without mishap. We always had two strong buckets with lanyards on the counter to be used as brakes when being towed into the locks. They were kicked over at just the right moment and were remarkably effective. Of course there were a few incidents; I remember Tommy Rose steering *If* into the lock at Cairnbaan under the watchful eye of the rather dour lockkeeper and going far too fast. He threw his stern line up and shouted "We have no reverse" - no response - again "We have no reverse!" the lockkeeper did not pick up the rope but simply turned his back. *If's* sharp bow made a neat triangular dent in the solid oak lock gate and Tommy was furious. "Why didn't you take my line?" he asked, to be met with the reply "Mr Rose, I do not take kindly to being told to get off my erse!"

Clyde puffer Anzac at Crinan

Once through the canal the whole of the west opens up before you. We almost always headed north from Crinan, but there are many interesting places on the west side of Kintyre. The islands of Islay and Jura have their attractions and the Clyde Cruising Club's annual "Classic Malts" cruise in company visits the distilleries there. Although I know both islands, for some reason we more often sailed to other islands such as Colonsay where I recall calm sunny days anchored and bathing at Kiloran Bay on the west side of the island. This is very much a temporary anchorage as it is completely exposed to the west, but on the occasions I was there the weather was amazing and the white clean sands were deserted. One could almost be on a remote tropical island. To sail to Colonsay from Crinan, the shortest route is through the Gulf of Corrievreckan between the islands of Jura and Scarba where the tide flows at 8 knots or more. This is perhaps the most notorious place on the west coast and the C.C.C. sailing directions warn yachtsmen to be extremely careful and not to attempt a passage with the flood in even moderate westerly winds. The gulf has a very uneven bottom which combined with the strong tidal stream produces a large whirlpool which can make a small boat completely helpless and at its mercy. Some of today's sailors are less cautious than in the past and a few take unnecessary risks in sailing through. Many years ago Andrew Tindal who owned *Aline* a Mylne designed 11 tonner was fascinated by the Corrievreckan and camped on Jura for a few weeks overlooking the whirlpool to study it. I do not know the outcome of his vigil but he had a healthy respect for it. Even in calm weather at slack water, there is a strange eeriness about this place and in a westerly gale on the flood the sea boils and roars so loudly it can be heard for miles.

Our more usual passage was through the Dorus Mor, past Pladda, up the Firth of Lorne heading for Mull. Unlike the Clyde where tides do not usually present a problem for yachts, the tides here are strong, particularly between islands or where the tidal stream flowing from the Irish sea is forced through the narrow channels to find its way north. Great care must be taken particularly in bad weather. For yachts under sail it is recommended to go through the Dorus Mor with the tide, although a boat with plenty of power can push through against it. I only once succeeded in making it against the flood in *Wye*, when we were desperate to get back to Crinan and arrived at the Dorus Mor (Great Door) just too late as the wind had been light on our passage south and the door was firmly shut! I had heard that it is possible to find an eddy off Craignish Point, The wind was southerly and we tacked close into the shore just before the point itself at the entrance to Loch Craignish. At first we seemed to make little headway over the ground, although we were moving furiously through the water with the sea boiling round us and whirlpools trying to spin us round. As we came closer to the point and picked up the eddy, we started to creep ahead. Short tacking around the point so close that we could almost step ashore, we squeezed our way through and managed to get to Crinan on time.

There are many interesting anchorages on the way, but also hazards. On one occasion in *Northward* we were slowly making our way south to Crinan when the visibility decreased to thick fog as we approached Sheep Island. With Harold navigating by dead reckoning, no G.P.S. or radar then! We slowly crept towards the shore until we recognised a landmark on Easdale. Suddenly we heard a foghorn and shouting and out of the fog a white yacht appeared. This was a German yacht from Hamburg, the *Ortac* a 20 ton Robert Clark designed cutter about the same size as *Northward* owned by a Hamburg based sailing club. They were quite lost and very worried as their pilot book had stern warnings about the tides. What a co-incidence! I had recently returned from Germany and as we came alongside I spoke to them in German much to their surprise. We towed them into Crinan as they had no engine and there was very little wind. Needless to say we had a great celebration which went on late into the night. It was really amazing that within a few years we had helped two well known German yachts in trouble in Scotland!

Come with me now on a fictional cruise, visiting some of my favourite places. We will simply try to explore a few of these to give you a taste of my experiences. Please forgive me if your favourite anchorage has been omitted.

On heading north from Pladda up the Sound of Scarba with the island of Luing to starboard we arrive at the north end of Luing, which is separated from Seil by the Cuan Sound. This is another notorious tidal area and boats have to be careful not to be swept onto rocks or the shore on passing through. The Cleit rock is clearly seen and helps the newcomer find his passage through which should only be attempted with the tide. Further up Seil Sound is the "Bridge over the Atlantic" at Clachan, straddling the weedy shallows of the sound which eventually opens out to the north close to Puilladobhrain. This is a popular anchorage, a short walk to the small hotel at Clachan called "Tigh na Truish" meaning the house of trousers in Gaelic. This was where highlanders changed from kilt to lowland dress when coming south after the defeat of the Jacobites at Culloden when highland dress was outlawed. Before leaving Luing, we always visited Irene McLachlan at Ardinamir on Luing which is a small bay sheltered by Torsa island to the north. Irene alas no longer with us, lived in her cottage at Ardinamir all her life. After the death of her father she continued to work her croft with her small herd of "Luing" cattle. Irene was a real character and never married but she took a keen interest in the visiting yachts of which there were hundreds, keeping a visitor's book with the names and dates of every boat that anchored at Ardinamir. On seeing the top of a mast approaching over Torsa, Irene would wait until the boat started to come in, then stand on the shore watching and bawling instructions to the crew in her inimitable way as they came through the entrance. The way in is tricky and many boats have stuck on the rock which although not marked was always pointed out vocally by Irene. "You're far too far to the south" or "No use heaving and carrying on, you'll be there until the next tide" were typical examples of her advice. Irene was made an honorary life-member of the Clyde Cruising Club but since her demise Ardinamir is no longer what it was.

Many yachtsmen visit Oban, the largest town on the West Coast but fewer go ashore on the island of Kerrera. I have a particular interest in this island as my late sister Joyce Glen lived at Ardentrive farm for many years. Her family still live there and we often visit them. For several years Joyce ran a bed and breakfast and provided evening meals for yachtsmen who moored at the boatyard. She had a visitor's book and it was interesting to see the names of visiting boats from different countries as Oban is such a busy tourist town in the summer months. Kerrera is situated directly opposite Oban. There are no roads or cars on the north end of the island but the inhabitants can be at the shops by boat in 10 minutes. Several of my nephews and nieces have made their lives on the island and David and Karen Keys run the farm and bed and breakfast as Joyce before them, while Scott Glen has an oyster farming business there. Karen has four children and it is good to see young people growing up in this environment, so different from the city way of life.

Our passage north usually takes us up the Sound of Mull to Tobermory and we will be visiting this delightful town later in this chapter. First though, I wish to take you to some of the places in the Firth of Lorne just across from Kerrera. Duart castle stands prominently on the south east corner of Mull and is the seat of the clan Maclean. The present chief, Sir Lachlan Maclean has a flat at the Castle and visitors can see round this imposing building and learn some of its history. Many violent deeds were committed in the past in Scotland and the story of the Lady Rock is typical of the grisly clan feuds of the times. Off Lismore there is a rock marked with a white beacon with an interesting history. An ancestor of the Maclean, Lachlan Cattenach Maclean married Lady Elizabeth Campbell who was a sister of the third Earl of Argyll. He had helped put down an insurrection led by the Maclean which perhaps led to what followed. Lady Elizabeth was barren and Maclean decided to get rid of her. He arranged for her to be tied to the rock at low water and left to drown as the tide rose. Some of her own clansmen the Campbells rescued her in the nick of time and took her to her brother at Inverary Castle. Maclean was later assassinated in Edinburgh by Sir John Campbell of Cawder.

We now leave Duart astern and sail round the south side of Mull. Heading south west down the Firth of Lorne we first pass Loch Spelve which is the only reasonable anchorage along this coast. With the rugged mountains and cliffs of the Ross of Mull to starboard we make our way south west to the Torran Rocks. These are dangerous waters with reefs and unmarked rocks. The passage must be made with great care and should be avoided in heavy weather or poor visibility. Once past the rocks we see the island of Earraid off the Ross of Mull. This island was immortalised in Sir Walter Scott's novel *Kidnapped* as the island where David Balfour was marooned after the brig *Covenant* was wrecked on the Torran Rocks. There is a popular little anchorage called Tinker's Hole there and another known as the Bull Hole in the Sound of Iona.

Iona Abbey cloisters

Once past Earraid, the island of Iona lies ahead. Much has been written about this place. Both spiritual and secular writers recognise that there is something special about Iona. Most people know that St. Columba brought Christianity to Scotland when he arrived on Iona in 563 A.D. He came over from Ireland in a currach, a primitive boat made of hides stretched over wicker frames along with twelve monks to build a chapel on the site where the abbey stands today. A monastery was founded and after Columba's death in 596 A.D. Iona remained the centre of Christianity in Scotland. Invasions and massacres by pagan Vikings caused the centre to be re-located to Scone during the reign of Kenneth MacAlpine but in 1203 Reginald, Lord of the Isles founded a Benedictine monastery on the island again. During the reformation much of the monastery was destroyed and it was only in 1899 that the 8th Duke of Argyll gifted it to the Church of Scotland and it was restored for public worship by 1905. The Rev. George MacLeod from Glasgow founded the Iona Community in 1938 and over many years the restoration of the other buildings was eventually completed. Pilgrims from many countries come to Iona each year and at times the island is quite crowded. The Abbey and monastery buildings are now in the safe hands of the National Trust for Scotland. I have visited Iona several times over the years. My mother was very fond of the island and we sometimes anchored in the Sound or at Bunessan to take the ferry across from Fionnphort on Mull. My father was friendly with Walter Tindal who farmed on the island and owned the Columba Hotel. I remember my first ride on a tractor when he took us all to the shell beach on the North West side of the island for a picnic. It was remarkable, instead of sand the beach consisted entirely of tiny shells, some almost as small as a grain of sand. Once the tourists leave for the last ferry to Mull the island is calm again. Although geographically and geologically similar to other islands in the Inner Hebrides, there is a Godly peace about Iona and it is a place where you feel truly in touch with your Creator. Just to sit on the top of Dun I, the highest point on the island watching the sun set in the west with the sound of seabirds in the air is one of life's great spiritual experiences.

Five miles north of Iona lies the half mile long island of Staffa where Fingals Cave inspired Mendelssohn to write his Hebridean Overture. He described the cave as "like the interior of a gigantic organ for the wind and waves to play on" Once you has been there and seen the huge basalt hexagonal columns like organ pipes and heard the sound of the sea breaking into the cave, you can understand exactly what he meant. It is not often that a yacht can anchor at Staffa as if is very exposed but it is worth waiting for a quiet day. We anchored there once in good weather and walked round to the cave from the landing place without all the tourists who flock in with the boat every day in the summer. Staffa is uninhabited apart from a few sheep.

Continuing north from Iona we sail past a number of interesting places on the west side of Mull. The village of Bunessan at the mouth of Loch Scridain is a popular anchorage for yachts. Colin and Jane Tindal run the exquisite Tiroran House Hotel near the head of the loch on the north side. Colin is a yachtsman and sailors are welcome in this lovely house and gardens where nautical photos and books abound. Loch na Keal is the next loch where Ben Mor dominates the landscape. Although beautiful, it is not a particularly popular destination for yachts, probably due to the distance from more accessible places. There are small anchorages on Ulva and Gometra and the Treshnish Isles but as usual in these parts one has to keep a sharp lookout for rocks. To the west lie the larger islands of Coll and Tiree. Tiree is a popular holiday island, very low lying with wonderful white sands. I know two Glasgow families who have been coming to Tiree every summer for their holidays for over 40 years. Nowadays, international windsurfing events are held there and at these times there is not a room to be had anywhere on the island. The only anchorage for yachts is at Gott bay on the south east side, near the village of Scarinish, but it is quite open and yachts more often anchor for the night at Arinagour in the neighbouring island of Coll. I remember evenings spent in the Coll Hotel where the host Alistair Oliphant entertained the guests with conjuring tricks and accordion. When asked once when the bar closed he replied

"October, or when the policeman comes over from Tiree, once he leaves after a dram we open again!"

We have now completed our short visit to the west coast of Mull and ease our sheets to a westerly breeze to run eastwards passing Cailiach and Ardmore Points to Tobermory. Sheltered by Calve Island, this is one of the most popular harbours in Scotland and is always a hive of activity. At the height of the season when West Highland Week is in progress, there can be a few hundred yachts in the bay. Some moorings are provided, but most boats anchor over on the west side where the water is shallower as it is too deep in the middle of the bay except for large vessels. At one time yachts vied with each other to be anchored as close as possible to the Mishnish Hotel, but a buoyed channel for fishing vessels has put a stop to that. The late Bobby McLeod, a world class accordion player of Scottish dance music owned the Mishnish Hotel and it was a great treat to listen to him playing in the bar at night. His son Robert continues to run the hotel and it is always busy with a large public bar packed with hundreds of thirsty sailors at regatta times.

Tobermory has prospered in recent years and I put it down to two things. Firstly land at the top of the bay has been reclaimed and made into a large bus and car park. Previously coach tours had problems in Tobermory as there was no room to turn a coach on the main street and the drivers were reluctant to reverse out of the village. Secondly and more importantly, Tobermory is known to thousands of children as Balamory which is a fictional children's' T.V. series set in the village using the actual brightly painted houses as sets.

This has brought a vast number of infants with their parents from all over the UK, who sometimes arrive with no accommodation booked and are surprised to find "no room at the inn". Some of the permanent residents of the houses featured in the programme are pestered so much by visitors, that they have been forced to leave home during busy times. It is rumoured that one resident whose door bell had rung for the umpteenth time in one day told the children that "Miss Hoolie had been murdered and was buried in the garden" Not very clever! Tears followed and angry parents threatened. The Balamory phenomenon has without doubt been a blessing to Mull and Tobermory in particular. All the shops seem busy and prosperous and there is a fresh confidence about the place which for many years seemed to be in decline. The Tobermory Galleon the *Florencia* is thought to be a survivor of the Spanish Armada which sailed north with an alleged cargo of gold bullion in 1588. In a dispute with the locals over the payment for stores the ship was blown up and is buried to this day in the soft mud at the bottom of the bay. Many attempts have been made to retrieve the treasure and I remember Alan Brown, who owned the ironmongers shop, now run by his nephew's widow Olive Brown, showing me a sword and cannon ball which had been recovered from the wreck. No gold has been found but doubtless a fresh attempt will be made someday as technology advances.

Tobermory

A popular port of call from Tobermory is the island of Canna. A day sail of around 30 miles with a fair wind and a good anchorage when you get there is reason enough for most. Canna is linked to Sanday at low water and between the islands you will find one of the most sheltered anchorages in the Hebrides. On approaching the anchorage from the east the compass may not show the correct bearing. This is due to the effect of Compass Hill which is situated on the eastern end of the island and has enough iron ore in the rock to affect ships' compasses. Most of the Hebrides are either firmly Catholic or Protestant and Canna remained Catholic after the reformation, although there is a delightful small Kirk near the anchorage which unfortunately is no longer used. A feature of visiting Canna in a yacht was to paint the yacht's name on the cliff face at the pier. We certainly painted our boats' names wherever we could find space and my father almost fell into the harbour once painting Tunnag in large white letters. I am not sure if this custom is still popular but it was fun to see who had been there before. John Lorne Campbell the Gaelic scholar, historian and farmer lived in Canna House the largest property on the island. Dr Campbell owned the world's largest library of Celtic language and literature which he donated along with Canna House to the National Trust for Scotland in 1981. He fought to keep the island intact as a viable community and made great efforts to prevent the island from becoming depopulated, Although Dr. Campbell did much good for Canna. I seem to remember that yachtsmen were not always welcome as some did not respect the peace and tranquillity of the island or the way of life of the islanders.

Across the Minch now to the "Long Isle" as the Outer Hebridean chain of islands is sometimes called. This is my favourite part of the West of Scotland. In all our boats we always tried to get out west although sometimes the weather prevented us. One of the most beautiful spots is the island of Vatersay situated just south of Barra. Now joined to Barra by a causeway, it was quite isolated until recent times. This was a blessing to visitors trying to get away from it all but a real problem for the local people trying to make a living there. Vatersay has exceptionally white sands on both the east and west sides of the island, separated by a few hundred yards of machair and dunes. The first time I landed there was in 1954 in *Tunnag* where we anchored in the clearest water and could easily see every detail on the bottom in 5 or 6 fathoms of water. We were in company with Ian Young and his family in *Arcturus*, the Watsons in *Mokoia*, Dr. Ken Young in *Vagrant II*, Jimmy Monaghan in *Nighan Donn*, as well as a few other C.C.C. yachts. The weather was perfect and we bathed in the clear water and picnicked on the perfect white sands on both beaches. The locals were quite amazed to see so many boats in at once and there were some wonderful white horses overlooking us on the hill to complete the picture. As Vatersay is close to Barra it was decided to take the yachting crowd over to Castlebay in *Tunnag*. This was hilarious with over 40 people aboard. We tied up at the pier and the adults all trooped into the pub which had featured in the book and film Whisky Galore. I remember an elderly lady enquiring politely as she saw us all coming ashore "Where do you all sleep?"

Barra is a larger island than Vatersay and also has white sands. The cockle beach serves as the airport runway and the timetables are set by the tides as planes can only land at low water when enough of the shore is uncovered. The village of Castlebay, made famous in the film "Whisky Galore" nestles below Heaval the highest hill on the island. This is a Norse name. There are many place names of Norse origin in the islands reminding us of the invasion and occupation of much of the west by the Vikings. The imposing Kisimul Castle, seat of the Clan McNeil stands solidly on a rock in the bay. The castle dates from the 11th Century and the present building was completed in the 15th century. A herald used to proclaim from the great tower each day - "Hear ye people and listen ye nations, the great McNeil of Barra having finished his meal, the princes of the earth may dine," such was his self importance! We met the 45th clan chief Robert Lister McNeil an American architect who had restored the castle and showed us round. When the chief is at home a flag flies from the tower. He died in 1970 and his son the 46th Chief is often in residence. Another time in *Flicka* with Vivien and the children we were snugly anchored in Castlebay when looking out to sea we saw a small sail approaching. The forecast was bad and we were a little curious about this boat. When it eventually arrived we saw it was a Wayfarer dinghy with three people aboard. They tied up alongside the pier and spread out their clothes to try and dry out. I went ashore and spoke to them to discover they were from Manchester. The crew consisted of a late middle aged man with his lady friend along with her teenage daughter. They had trailed the boat up to Oban by road and wanted to sail to Mingulay but thought they should first stop at Barra. They had no idea of navigation and very little knowledge of sailing. The young girl was terrified and they were all completely soaked. They were not even wearing life jackets when they arrived. We took pity on them as the weather was deteriorating fast and invited them all aboard for a meal. After dinner it was too wild to attempt to row ashore so they stayed for the night squeezing into the aft cabin, while our kids doubled up with us. The man in particular seemed oblivious to the dangers of crossing the Minch in a dinghy without lifejackets, charts or even a good compass. I just hope they got back home safely after we left them.

Next morning the weather was still bad and on getting our anchor up, as we wanted to move to a more sheltered berth our anchor buoy line fouled the propeller. We heaved and pulled, turning the engine over slowly forward and astern but if was firmly stuck. Suddenly the line went slack and we pulled it up to find the propeller attached to it much to our surprise and delight. A diver was found in the village and the prop refitted the next morning.

Sailing north again we pass a few small islands to port – Fulay, Flodday, Hellisay, Gighay and Fuday which would be interesting to explore in settled weather but we usually anchor in Acarsaid Mhor in Eriskay which is reasonably secure but difficult to enter or leave due to the sunken rocks. I described the entrance in chapter 4. I also mentioned that Prince Charlie landed at on the west side from France in 1745, which was the first time he had been on Scottish soil. A species of pink sea convolvulus grows amongst the grass on the dunes above the beach and legend has it that "Prince Charlie's Flower" came from seeds dropped by him as he came ashore. It is also claimed that these pink flowers are only found in this place. Eriskay also has its ponies, which are a distinctive Scottish breed, used over the centuries for carrying peat and seaweed. The small population is mainly Roman Catholic and I remember meeting an old lady still living in one of the traditional black houses who said her life was complete as she had been introduced to the Queen when she visited Eriskay in *Britannia*.

Eriskay is famous as the "Whisky Galore Island." In 1941 the 12,000 ton steamship *SS Politician* bound for New York from Liverpool was wrecked in the Sound of Eriskay with a cargo of 264,000 bottles of whisky! The story is well known and much of the cargo had disappeared by the time the customs officers arrived to deal with the situation. Bottles were hidden all over the island and some even turned up many years later still intact. Sir Compton McKenzie wrote his hilarious book followed by the film, but omitted to include the fact that nineteen islanders were prosecuted and imprisoned at Inverness. In 1988 although Eriskay had always been a "dry island" the first pub was opened. Named appropriately "Am Politician" I believe they have a few bottles of the original Polly drams on display. They are now undrinkable as sea water contaminated the whisky through the cork, as corks were used at that time for whisky bottles before screw tops were introduced.

Back across the Minch we visit anchorages in and around the Isle of Skye. One of my favourites is South Rona just north of Raasay. Not to be confused with North Rona which is over 100 miles away in the North Atlantic, South Rona is a completely deserted island which was inhabited until 1919. The reason for the population leaving the island is thought to be the scarcity of water. The island is rocky and treeless and it is difficult to imagine anyone trying to make a living there as working the land would seem to be almost impossible. I remember as a child visiting South Rona and exploring the old village. Many of the cottages were still standing and there were even items left in some. There were bibles in the church pews and slates on the schoolhouse desks. It was as if the people had suddenly disappeared into thin air. The anchorage Acarsaid Mor on the west side is very sheltered, indeed the world voyaging yachtsman Eric Hiscock described it as the best small boat anchorage he had ever visited when he cruised here in *Wanderer III*.

Sailing south down the Inner Sound, we leave Raasay and Scalpay to starboard turning eastwards into Loch Carron to the delightful village of Plockton. Avoiding the Hawk Rock and other hazards we anchor in one of the most pleasant anchorages on the mainland. Plockton is cheerful village with clean colourful cottages along the main street and even a few palm trees in the gardens. There is a continental atmosphere about the place and it is easy to feel one is miles away from the West of Scotland particularly when the sun shines. Plockton has also been a T.V. location, the Hamish McBeth series was made here. The village looks across Loch Carron to the hills to the east and there is a fleet of attractive open clinker built sailing boats which race regularly in the loch.

On leaving Plockton – carefully – one tends to be casual about rocks when leaving an anchorage and much more careful on arriving, we continue south under the Skye bridge into Loch Alsh leaving Kylakin to starboard and Lyle of Lochalsh to port. The next destination is Totaig in Loch Duich. Some consider this to be the most beautiful anchorage in the entire West and certainly the view of the Kintail hills with Eilean Donan castle is spectacular; much better seen in real life than the popular view often shown in calendars and postcards. When we visited Totaig in *Northward* we met Jimmy (Jimmack) Jeffrey, the skipper of *Kismet* moored there. *Kismet* is one of the few 15 metre racing yachts in the world. Built by Fife in 1909, 75ft over all length and originally named *Tiuga*, she had been converted from her original gaff to bermudan rig. The owner had died but his widow kept the yacht for sentimental reasons. Jimmy and his young crew were retained and lived aboard in fine style as the lady only went for a sail perhaps once a year! As Jimmy was a very large gentleman we were convinced that his ample girth was caused by easy living and no exercise. He had a fine line in stories of his racing days and could entertain us for hours. *Kismet* was eventually sold to Ian Rose who had previously owned the 8 Metre *June* and re-named her *Nevada*. He stepped a spare aluminium mast from the 12 Metre *Sceptre* in her and cruised and raced her for a few years on the Clyde. After Ian sold her, I believe she went to the Mediterranean and was eventually found and restored by Fairlie Restorations in 1992 to her original rig and condition. Now named *Tuiga* again, she is based in Monaco and races in the various classic regattas in the Med. Other 15 metre yachts - *The Lady Anne* also by Fife has been rebuilt and the *Hispania* will soon be relaunched to join them. Jimmy Jeffrey, also known as the "Monsoon Puddock," retired to Port Bannatyne and many yachtsmen will remember his stories over a pint in the "Anchor Inn" where Malcolm MacMillan was the host. He would tell yarns of his youth, when he raced in 12 and 6 Metres and many other yachts. In common with so many of his generation and background he was a real seaman with a great knowledge and feel for boats and the sea.

Sailing boats at Plockton

There are many places which we could visit on our way south but I want to mention Loch Scavaig in particular. I told of our experiences there in Northward in 1959 in chapter 2 and I have been there several times since. Like many west coast anchorages the entrance can be tricky but it is worth the effort. The loch is an almost landlocked pool with the Cuillins rising directly up from the water giving a somewhat sinister atmosphere. Even in high summer the sun only shines into the anchorage for a short time due to the height of the surrounding mountains. Sudden squalls can come on unsuspecting sailing boats and yachts under sail should be extremely careful in northerly winds. One feels so insignificant in this place; a small speck on the landscape and the remoteness and wildness is overpowering especially if alone. One year in *Northward* we were sheltering from a westerly gale there. The weather was awful with strong winds and continual rain but we were quite snug as we lay there for two days until the weather improved. We could see a small tent high up on the mountain and wondered how on earth the people were coping. We felt really sorry for them as we assumed they were trying to find shelter in it. On walking ashore Harold met the young couple who were the occupants. Their first words were that they were sorry for us! "It must be terrible being cooped up in a small boat in this weather" they said! We brought them aboard and fed them as they had not had a hot meal for several days and everything in their tent was completely soaked. They were amazed how comfortable we were; they had simply no idea what a yacht is like below. They stayed aboard for the night and went back to climb mountains again in the morning.

Before returning to Crinan and home waters we will call in at Rum the largest of the small isles. Rum is owned by the Nature Conservancy Council and visitors although not prohibited are not exactly encouraged. There is a large herd of red deer on Rum and wild goats, highland cattle and Rum ponies (supposedly having been brought on ships of the Spanish Armada) populate the island which is very mountainous. Rum is also a mecca for bird watchers and large colonies of Manx Shearwaters breed in the peaks. The Norse place names remind us that these islands only became part of Scotland again in 1263 when the Vikings were defeated. The greatest surprise on Rum is Kinloch Castle. This imposing building faces Loch Scresort which is the only anchorage on the island. This red sandstone Edwardian mansion was built by Sir George Bullough in 1900. London architects and red sandstone from Arran with stone masons from Lancashire all combined with extravagant interior decoration to produce a spectacular building. The workmen were paid a penny a day extra to wear kilts and tuppence a day for tobacco to ward off midges! A prime example of Edwardian opulence, there were even live turtles and alligators in heated tanks and air conditioning in the billiard room to remove cigar smoke. There were "Jacuzzi" type baths and a remarkable mechanical "orchestrian" which still works, operated by punched paper rolls just like a massive musical box playing military marches Strauss waltzes and many other pieces with trumpets, drums and other instruments. Although the castle was closed when we were there, the caretaker kindly showed us round and played the orchestrian for us. The castle has recently been the subject of a T.V. programme about the restoration of old buildings and it is hoped that funds will be forthcoming to bring Kinloch back to its former glory.

Leaving Rum astern we head south to round Ardnamurchan Point, the most westerly point of the Scottish mainland. I have seen it in wild weather when the Atlantic swell combined with wind and tide make it a most unpleasant place to be in a small yacht and I have also been there when the sea was like polished glass. The granite lighthouse tower, like all the other lighthouses no longer manned, stands clearly out on the point showing us the way to go home. Just north of Ardnamurchan Point is Sanna bay which is a sheltered anchorage in southerly winds. It is not advisable to stay too long in these parts, as the weather can change very quickly and it is better to be south of Ardnamurchan before it breaks. Loch Moidart is another beautiful loch nearby but not so often visited. A tricky entrance with many rocks, care must be taken but the anchorage is pretty and sheltered near the ruined Castle Tioram once stronghold of the MacDonalds of Clanranald dating from the 14th Century.

Once past Ardnamurchan most yachts head straight for the fleshpots of Tobermory but there is Loch Sunart to explore. This is a long loch with the perfect anchorage of Loch Drumbuy near the mouth and the islands of Oronsay and Carna. Most yachts do not have the time or inclination to venture to the head of the loch but it is worth a visit. My father in law Colin Lang in *Nomad II* motoring up the loch once at six knots accidentally hit a rock or "brick" as he called it. Fortunately the damage was not too bad and they got back to Crinan safely for repairs. In the Sound of Mull Loch Aline is also worth exploring, most boats anchor at the mouth of the loch but a sail up to the head is interesting. In 1989 my father aged 78 with Harold 80 along with my nephews Stuart and Scott both teenagers, were cruising in our yawl *Macaria*. They were anchored in Loch Aline during a severe summer gale. With both anchors and all their chain out they rode out the storm but at home we were very worried as we had not heard from them for several days and they could not contact us.

We are now almost back in home waters on our fictional cruise. I hope you have enjoyed our short visit. There are many interesting places to see without going as far as the Outer Isles or north of Skye. Many yachts are based north of Crinan nowadays. Cruibh Haven, Dunstaffinage, Ardfern and Crinan are all popular marinas and mooring places and most people find the two hour car journey from Glasgow no obstacle to enjoying the peace of the west. Although there are many more yachts in commission today than in my youth there is still plenty of room. It is true that in the summer holiday season although some of the popular anchorages are full of boats, there are many more which are unspoiled and quiet. It is truly one of the last wildernesses in Europe and easily accessible. Just the weather!!!!! We console ourselves with the thought that if the sun was always shining Scotland would be so overcrowded that we would not want to return.

Chapter 7 - Classic Yachts

When I grew up in the fifties and sixties almost all yachts were built of wood and each had its own characteristics. You could identify any boat much more easily than today and my brother Kenneth with excellent eyesight was known for his ability to recognise one from "miles away". Many of the boats on the Clyde at that time were locally built and yachts by famous designers – Milne, Fife and McGruer boats were commonplace. McGruer's yard at Clynder, Alex Robertson and Morris & Lorimer at Sandbank, Fairlie Yacht Slip, (successors to William Fife) as well as Bute Slip Dock were still building new wooden boats. I remember with pleasure wandering around McGruer's yard in those years watching the building progress of the latest Cruiser 8 (International 8 Metre Cruiser Racer Class). It was wonderful, the smell of the timber, teak and mahogany, pine and oak and the sight of partly completed hulls. Each time we were in the yard we would follow the progress from keel laying to the frames and planking and finally the launch. During these years McGruer's built a significant number of boats, most of which I remember well. These were mainly designed by James McGruer. From the fifties onwards these include the 8 Metre Cruiser/Racer class yachts, *Sonda, Josephine IV, Adastra X, Nahmara, Nan of Clynder, Orana, Camelia of Rhu, Gigi of Clynder, Debbie (Fionnuala), Feolinn, Inismara, Orani, Nan of Gare, Altricia* and *Debbie*. Cruising yachts included *Celaeno, Seonella, Dochas* and *Sally of Kames* (8 ton sloops), *Sule Skerry, Westward of Clynder, Marguerita Helena III* and *Coigach* (17 ton yawls), *Elona* (14 ton yawl), , *Wind of Lorne, Wind of Clynder, Nymph of Lorne, Teko, Elfin of Lorne* and *Malindi* (7 ton Lorne class*) Stornoway* (13 ½ metre CR), *Deb* (16 ton sloop), *Gabrielle III* (24 ton sloop*), Rinamara* (20 ton yawl), *Tritsch Tratsch* (18 ton IOR sloop), *Gosling* (Int. 6 metre), *Tritsch Tratsch II* (29 ton IOR sloop), *Kyla II* (16 ton sloop), *Talisker of Lorne* (10 ton sloop) and *Nippie Sweetie* (IOR ¾ tonner).

The McGruer business dates back to the late 1800's when Ewing McGruer started building boats at Rutherglen, a suburb of Glasgow. He was one of seven brothers and in turn produced seven sons. The business moved to Clynder on the Gareloch in the 1920's and it grew and prospered. Many famous yachts were built there including our old yacht *Northward*, which was the largest boat built by McGruers up to 1930. The seven sons were John, Ewing, Willie, James, Davie, Andrew and Alex. I knew Willie, James and Alex best. James was the designer, Alex looked after the yard and slipways and Willie was the front man who spoke to the customers. I remember my father being quite exasperated as he had not received a bill from McGruers for two years. It eventually arrived and full of indignation with many questions about its content, he raced down to Clynder. On being greeted by Willie who was a master of diplomatic charm his anger melted and all was well. It was always a mystery to us how they could afford to send out bills so infrequently.

In those days the yachts on the Clyde were all "classic" by today's definition and wooden yachts were the norm. I remember the first glassfibre boat on the Clyde which was *Shadow* owned by John Simpson. She was followed by *Siolta,* owned by John McKean which was an Excalibur to replace his pretty Milne designed 18 ton cutter which he had sold to Iceland. We were died in the wool traditionalists and viewed these new boats with considerable scepticism. At the time it was hard to believe that this was the future and that 40 years later the great majority of yachts would be built in this material. I have nothing against G.R.P. as a boat building material, as it has many advantages but I am dismayed by many of today's designs. It seems that comfortable accommodation and interior facilities are sometimes considered more important than seaworthiness or visual appearance. I have always put great store on the look of a yacht, perhaps I am old fashioned, but as I go sailing for pleasure, my boat has to appeal to me visually to provide the satisfaction of ownership. One old yachtsman once described today's marina occupiers as "like Ford cars in a car park". No doubt production boats have enabled many more people to take up sailing but it is always a mystery to me why even in the finest weather, so many are tied up in their berths and so few actually out sailing. Marinas have also in my opinion led to a lack of seamanship and many of the skills which every yachtsman learned in the past are rarely used today. These include – manoeuvring under sail, picking up moorings, rowing a proper dinghy and even the simple task of anchoring.

Now I have got this off my chest I can return to the subject of classic boats. My generation were fortunate indeed to have experienced the old Clyde yachting scene before it changed for ever. There were still several large yachts around when we had *Northward* some of these were *Vadura* -109 ton Milne ketch owned by James Howden Hume, *Mariella* - 74 ton Fife built yawl owned by Ronald Teacher, *Griselda* - 80 ton Fife yawl owned by Oswald Graham and *Roska* - 62 ton Milne gaff ketch owned by Mr. McGeorge. Others included *Mingary* - 34 ton Milne ketch, *Eilidh*

- 30 ton Milne cutter, the Fife 12 Metre *Cerigo, Seewolf - 34* ton German built ketch and *Cruinnaig III* – 47 ton Dickie built ketch. I also admired the Le Havre pilot cutter *Leonora* owned by retired Captain Cameron who sailed alone with his paid hand and *Hirta* the Bristol Channel Pilot Cutter owned by Adam Bergius. I have always had a special affection for this type of working boat and my father and I at one time seriously considered buying *Hirta* from Adam Bergius but the head eventually ruled the heart when we realised how big a commitment such a vessel would be. *Leonora* is now back at Le Havre with her original name *Marie Fernand* but *Hirta* is currently awaiting restoration after few traumatic years and changes of ownership following the yachting author Tom Cunliffe's successful cruises in her. As keen youngsters we were always disappointed that the big yachts did not sail more often as they were usually seen under power. It seemed that in those with paid crews the skippers were good at giving the owners all the reasons why it was better to leave the sail covers on! On a Saturday evening two or three could usually be seen anchored at the Burnt Islands in the Kyles of Bute where bridge parties were held aboard. The one time in the season they all raced was the annual Clyde Corinthian Yacht Club's Tarbert Race, when it was wonderful to see them really sailing competitively. During these years most people assumed that this was the end of the big yacht era but life is full of surprises; the unexpected can happen as time would tell.

Mariella

In recent years there has been an explosion of interest worldwide in classic and traditional yachts. The "Old Gaffers Association" was formed 25 years ago to encourage and provide a platform for traditional gaff rig. Today it flourishes and holds many events around the British Isles and elsewhere. The number of gaff rigged yachts has increased contrary to predictions in the sixties when it looked as if it would completely die out. Owners with new boats as well as old, some in G.R.P are O.G.A. members. There have been and continue to be many restorations of old wooden yachts all over the world. Famous boats by Fife, Milne, Nicholson, G.L. Watson and others have been rescued, sometimes as wrecks or houseboats and restored at great expense by wealthy owners. A Fife yacht is now a collector's piece and some are very valuable. "Classic Boat" magazine which recently celebrated its 200th issue has helped kindle this interest and revival in classic and traditional boats which is growing all over Europe and worldwide.

After my various glassfibre boats – *Muchacha, Skulmartin* and *Flicka*, I was without a yacht for several years until one day visiting Crinan with my father, we noticed a little black painted gaff yawl at Crinan Harbour. My father said she reminded him of his old boat *Ron*. I said I think she's for sale. To my surprise he replied "Why don't I buy her and teach my grandchildren to sail in a real boat?" I replied "Why not, I will do all the work!" As my father had sold his last boat the Giles ketch *Fabella* some years before I was somewhat surprised but delighted as I was unable at that time to go it alone. He bought *Macaria* a 1922 Peter Dickie designed canoe stern gaff yawl. At 9 tons T.M. and 34 feet overall she was sound and virtually unaltered over the years. After a survey we started a programme of work to bring her up the best condition possible. Although there were no major problems she had not been used much in the previous years and there were many jobs to do. Many people today find it hard to understand why people want to own an old wooden boat. The usual remark is "What a lovely boat but what a lot of work!" It is true that old boats need a lot of work to bring them up to a high standard but regular annual maintenance is not a chore if you enjoy it. It is very satisfying to see the boat improve as a result of your efforts. We scraped off all the paint and varnish and refinished topsides, bottom and brightwork. *Macaria* has beautiful teak hatches and skylights. The pitch pine bottom planking was so fresh after 70 years that resin still oozed from it when the paint was removed. We also re-finished the original mahogany interior panelling. Other work over the years we had her included new sails, a new Volvo engine, some re-fastening as well as new rigging and blocks. From 1989 to 1997 we had many good weekends and holidays in her and my father sailed in her regularly into his eighties until his death in 1994.

One of the highlights each year was the Portaferry Regatta in Northern Ireland. This event was originally for Galway Hookers, the traditional West of Ireland workboats, many of which have been restored but many other traditional boats took part. We first sailed over for this event in 1992 and Ian Young joined us in *Arcturus*. The weekend was hilarious, the Irish hospitality amazing and we made many new friends. We raced around Strangford Loch and managed to get a prize just beating the crack Galway Hooker skipper Jonnie Hellion in his *Morning Star*. One amusing incident is worth recalling. As we were reaching to the first mark and in the lead we could not see the buoy anywhere. We thought we had missed it and there is nothing worse than being in the lead and missing the mark! Just as we were despairing, an inflatable boat overtook us towing a large orange buoy and about a few cables ahead of us anchored it shouting "sorry we're late!" There were traditional boats of all types there and since then such events have grown in Ireland and the Isle of Man. They are great fun and I recommend then to anyone either with a suitable boat or just to go for the fun.

Macaria

For our first season in *Macaria* we moored at Crinan Harbour. One day I got a phone call from Nick Ryan, owner of the Crinan Hotel to tell me that an American film crew were at his hotel to take advertising photographs for Timberland Shoes. They had seen *Macaria* at Crinan and wanted to know if we would allow them to use the boat for their shots. I spoke to the chief photographer on the phone and after some negotiation with misunderstandings between pounds sterling and U.S. dollars we agreed a figure for a weekend charter. Their idea was for us to sail to Tobermory for filming there and then to return to Crinan for more pictures. Nick's daughter Julia was to model Timberland's new range of deck shoes and we would be finished by Sunday evening. It all seemed straightforward enough and my brother in law, John Glen and I took *Macaria* up to Tobermory on the Friday ready to start work on Saturday morning. We had a wild beat up the Sound of Mull but arrived in Tobermory unscathed. On meeting the Americans the first comment was "can you take away the little mast at the back? It will be in the way!" This was received with the contempt it deserved and I assured them that if we removed it we would be unable to sail! Once over this hurdle the camera crew came aboard, there were unbelievably six of them including a make up girl; all to take a few pictures for an advertisement! They all stood at the stern while Julia posed in various positions wearing the shoes. The joke was that they only had one pair and they were too small for Julia! We then were asked to sail around Tobermory bay and up and down the Sound of Mull while they took photos from Nick's boat *Scarbh*. We were then told to be available to sail again at 5.00AM the next morning; "to get the best light" they said, so the pantomime continued for the whole weekend. Eventually the problem with Julia's shoe size was addressed by flying another model in from London. It was apparently easier to get another model regardless of cost than another pair of shoes! The model girl arrived by car from Glasgow Airport to Crinan and was asked to get aboard *Macaria* from a dinghy several times until they got a good shot. The poor girl had never been in a boat before and probably never been much out of London and she was terrified of the water. By the end of the weekend they seemed happy enough though and were last seen finishing a substantial seafood dinner at the hotel while John and I had sandwiches in the bar. The film crew had been in Scotland for six weeks, staying at the best hotels and living well. I made contact with Timberland later but found out that none of the photos were used although they must have taken hundreds! I was happy though the fees paid for our new sails.

We had many good times in *Macaria* and at that time I started a small business selling traditional fittings and equipment for classic boats. I called this business "Classic Marine" but due to other business commitments I sold it after three years to Moray McPhail who still trades from Woodbridge in Suffolk. It was at this time that I met the naval architect David Raeburn. We got on well and we both felt that due to the growing interest in classics, there was an opportunity to build classic style boats using modern building methods. This lead to our forming the company "Clyde Classics Ltd" and we decided to build a boat on spec. The design brief was for a yacht similar in size and rig to *Macaria* but with more beam, lighter displacement and better accommodation. David produced an attractive design and we rented a shed in Dumbarton where the first "Tarbert Yawl" was built in wood epoxy construction with the help of a Scottish Enterprise Innovative Development Grant. The strip planking was in cedar with diagonal mahogany veneers, overlaid with a glass cloth skin. The hull was immensely strong and the yacht was finished in a dark green epoxy coating. We employed several experienced boat builders and joiners and completed the job in six months from laying out the lines. There was a strict deadline as we had booked a stand with financial assistance from Dunbartonshire Enterprise at the London Boat Show and the boat had to be at Earl's Court before Christmas. We launched her at Dumbarton on a day when snow and sleet were falling and Paul Jeffries of T.S. Rigging of Maldon came up to fit all the hand spiced rigging. David and I were satisfied that she was floating to her marks and she was then taken by road to London for the show.

At Earl's Court our new boat was well received by the public and the yachting press. We had over 3,000 visitors aboard during the week and the magazines - in particular "Classic Boat" gave us good coverage. In fact Robin Gates the editor of "Classic Boat" featured the whole story of designing and building the Tarbert Yawl in four consecutive issues. It was somewhat to our surprise therefore when the eventual purchaser Ian Fleming came from Scotland. Named *Fynelyne,* she came back home and is now based in Skye. The boat was a great success and we had the opportunity to sail in her many times with her new owner, taking her over to Portaferry for the Traditional Boat Weekend. We also took her down to Cowes for the Cowes Classics regatta where she attracted a lot of interest and Beken took some excellent photos of her.

Clyde Classics had several other orders including the fit out of a Saga 40 G.R.P. hull in mahogany and teak to a high standard for a German client. We designed and built a classic motor launch for the large Milne ketch *Thendara* which was being restored at Southampton. We also rebuilt and restored the Milne designed ½ rater *Thistle* (now *Trix*) for a French owner and designed and built a 36 foot yacht for a Clyde yachtsman similar in concept to my old yacht *Flicka*. This was a light displacement fast cruising yacht with a wing keel, but with classic above water lines. *Starglint* was a fast and pretty yacht but we had many problems in building her. The last boat to be completed was a "Silverette" style motor yacht built as all the others in wood epoxy but with a clear varnished finish. David and I had been to Hamburg to discuss the possibility of building several boats for charter work on the Swiss Lakes. Unfortunately the deal fell through and Clyde Classics had to cease trading for financial reasons; as someone once said the most important boat building material is money! It was very sad and a difficult time for us. I realise in hindsight that it is virtually impossible to cost one-off boats effectively unless one has many years of experience. Every job we did was different and each had its own particular problems. It was perhaps also a lesson that it is sometimes unwise to try and turn your hobby into a business.

In 1992 I was invited to join *Cintra* the oldest 12 Metre afloat at the Nioulargue Regatta at St. Tropez. I had supplied Giorgetti & Magrini the Italian yard that restored *Cintra* with some fittings and I was delighted to be invited. When I arrived at St. Tropez, I was amazed to see a huge fleet of large classic yachts moored stern on to the quay in the heart of the old port. The usual berth holders had been moved out for the week! It was simply breathtaking to see so many beautiful yachts together. They were all immaculate with freshly varnished teak brightwork, polished brass fittings and spotless scrubbed decks. Since the last of the big boats left the Clyde, I had never imagined that I would see such yachts again. Walking along the quay I saw the famous "J" Class *Endeavour*, the 23 metres *Candida* and *Astra*, the schooners *Adix*, *Altair*, *Creole*, *Shenandoah*, *Puritan*, *Lelantina* and *Mariette* along with the ketches *Royona* and *Karenita*. Former Clyde Fife yachts *Solway Maid* and *Madrigal* as well as Eric Tabarly's *Pen Duick* and many others along with a dozen 12 Metres and numerous smaller yachts. What an amazing sight!

I found *Cintra* moored alongside the other 12 Metres, the Nicholson designed *Tomahawk* and the famous Stephens designed *Vim*. It transpired that all three yachts were owned by an Italian count and professionally crewed, kitted out in smart white trousers and red sweatshirts. I made myself known and soon discovered that practically no-one aboard spoke English and I know no Italian. We got on fine though and I joined the crew for dinner ashore at an expensive San Tropez restaurant. It became apparent that they dined this way every night at the owner's expense. This was yachting as I had never experienced it before! *Cintra* was designed by William Fife III and built at Fairlie in 1909. She had beautifully rebuilt with her original rig and is a fine example of a vintage racing gaff cutter.

We got underway in the morning along with all the other boats trying to get out of the harbour at once. Amidst the bustle and confusion it seemed that some of these expensive boats would get damaged but all was well and we were soon hoisting our huge mainsail followed by the topsail, jib, staysail and jib topsail. We were to sail in a different class from the other 12's as *Cintra* is gaff rigged and we found ourselves competing with *Pen Duick*. Communication on board was to say the least, interesting. Only one of the crew seemed to speak a little English but his girlfriend was with him and she was English. This was a relief for me and I managed to get a position aft on the counter looking after the topmast backstays. We started was along with the other 12 Metres although in a different class and we crossed the line in company with *Vim, Tomahawk, Sovereign, Columbia, Trivia, Flica II* and the rest in a 20 knot breeze. On the first windward leg I was interested to see that our boat speed was just as fast as the bermudan rigged 12 Metres and we rounded the mark in the midst of the fleet. Our course then took a different direction and we set a huge masthead spinnaker. There were some anxious moments when a hard squall hit us, as from the deck the topmast looked flimsy, but all the gear held and we tore off downwind with the rig intact. At the mark we had a good lead over Eric Tabarly in *Pen Duick* until our navigator made a mistake in identifying the next mark. We were happily reaching along when saw *Pen Duick* to our weather hard on the wind. We luffed up and to our dismay *Pen Duick* was now ahead. Nevertheless we gave chase and overhauled her after two more legs of the course but unfortunately not enough to save our time.

Cintra racing at St Tropez

For the next race we set our enormous jackyard topsail and jib topsail as the wind was lighter. We started on port tack with an assortment of large and extremely expensive yachts heading towards us on starboard. Our brave helmsman neatly luffed round the stern of one of the 12's and we got away in clean air from the rest of the fleet bunched up at the line. Once we tacked we were well ahead of all the other boats and it became one of those rare races when everything worked to perfection. *Pen Duick* was well astern in the middle of the fleet surrounded by other boats. Our spinnaker went up and down without problems. We tacked and covered other boats, avoiding getting under the lee of any of them and best of all our lead steadily increased. We finished 16 minutes ahead of *Pen Duick* after 13½ miles and felt confident of victory but were shattered to learn later that Eric had beaten us on corrected time.

After the race, moored back in St. Tropez the crew all got very excited and started changing into clean white trousers. I asked what was going on and received the answer "The boss, he come!" Suddenly a large black Mercedes with heavily tinted windows drove slowly along the quayside stopping where *Cintra, Vim* and *Tomahawk* were all moored together. The chauffeur opened the back door and a man wearing dark glasses with a camel coat hung loosely over his shoulders stepped out. It was like something out of "The Godfather". He shook hands with all three skippers, exchanged a few words, went back into the car and left. This was apparently the owner's annual visit to his yachts! I later learned that a large motor yacht with tinted windows which I had noticed close to us during the race was his "gin palace" from which he watched his yachts race. How the other half live indeed!

Perhaps my favourite yacht of all time is the 161 ton, 109 foot long gaff schooner *Altair*. Designed by William Fife III she was built in 1931 at Fairlie in teak for Captain Guy McCaw to cruise to the South Pacific. In 1986 *Altair* underwent a complete and authentic restoration at Southampton Yacht Services. The work was done to the highest standards and with great attention to detail. Even her sails which were made by Ratsey and Lapthorn were of specially dyed Dacron to simulate the exact colour of the original Egyptian cotton sails. *Altair* returned to the Clyde for her 60th birthday in 1991 and Archie McMillan who had taken over the Fife yard after the war as Fairlie Yacht Slip enjoyed sailing again on the yacht he helped to build 60 years before.

Altair was anchored off Largs Marina at that time and as my father and I were going aboard *Macaria* one day there was crowd at the end of the pontoon waiting to go aboard *Altair*. One person was looking closely at *Macaria* when we arrived and in a slight European accent asked us about our boat. We had a pleasant conversation. I asked him about *Altair* and told him how much we admired her. I then asked "Who is the owner of *Altair?*" He quietly replied "Actually I am!" He then introduced himself before boarding a beautiful vanished motor launch to go aboard. When I saw *Altair* at St. Tropez I decided to take the bull by the horns. I approached the gangway and asked if the owner was on board. The bare footed boy went forward to the main hatch to speak to him and a few minutes later he appeared. He remembered me from the previous year at Largs and invited me aboard. A girl with a tray of champagne filled glasses appeared and offered me one. We chatted for a few minutes before I plucked up enough courage to ask if I could possibly join the crew for a day. He simply said "You will have to ask Steve" and called Steve Hammond, the skipper. I had also met him at Largs and he is a very experienced yacht skipper. He simply said "Be here at 08.00 tomorrow morning". This was a dream come true. If I had been told 30 years before that I would be sailing on *Altair* in the company of some of the world's finest and largest classic yachts I would never have believed it. *Altair's* owner founded Fairlie Restorations on the Hamble about this time to restore and rebuild Fife yachts. Under Duncan Walker's management, a team of craftsmen produce the highest quality work and have already restored many Fife yachts including the 15 Metres *Tuiga* and *The Lady Anne*, the 8 Metres *Fulmar* and *Siris*, the 19 Metre *Marequita* and the gaff ketch *Kentra* amongst others.

Altair

I was up early that day and the weather was perfect. I walked down from my small hotel and had breakfast in one of the cafes overlooking the harbour where all the crews were getting ready. Decks were being scrubbed, varnish work dried off and brass polished. Most of the crews are young in these boats, mainly in their twenties, both male and female. The atmosphere was very international as the boats came from all over the world - the U.K., France, Italy, Germany, Greece, Australia and the U.S.A. At 08.00 I went aboard *Altair* and Steve introduced me to the rest of the crew. There would be about twenty on board that day of which seven were permanent crew. Most of them had been aboard for that season or longer and really knew the boat. Steve explained to me and the other visitors that we must not touch any line without being given an order, as on such a large boat with heavy gear it could be very dangerous if someone let off a halyard or topping lift by mistake. We set all sail, gaff mainsail and foresail with their topsails, staysail, jib and jib topsail. The main topsail was a jackyarder with yards like an 8 Metre's mast and boom! The wind was force three to four and the sun was shining - perfect conditions. Steve was at the helm and we had a good start amongst the most spectacular fleet I had ever seen. Just after the start we were overhauled by the three masted schooners *Creole* and *Adix* to weather and the huge *Candida* and *Astra* on our lee. *Endeavour* was well in the lead and we were surrounded by the other big boats. On the first leg which was a reach, the owner who had been down below at the start came on deck and I overheard him remark to Steve at the helm, "How are we doing Steve? I do not know why I'm here, I don't like racing" I also noticed one of the lady passengers sitting on the counter reading a paperback, seemingly oblivious to the incredible scene around us!

After an exciting couple of hours the wind gradually died away and it became obvious that we would not finish before dark. We were on the last leg broad reaching back to St. Tropez when darkness fell and with it the wind increased. We were under all our light weather sails – mainsail, foresail, main jackyard topsail, gollywobbler (large light fisherman's staysail set between the masts) and an enormous spinnaker. We were speeding up as the wind increased and it was becoming impossible to see where the finishing line was as the committee boat was in the shadow of the land. Steve at the helm called them up on the hand held V.H.F. and asked them to send up a flare so we could see the line. There were also dozens of speedboats, small yachts and other obstructions on the course making matters even more difficult. Steve was completely cool and calm. We sped across the line and the crew got all the sail off in a matter of minutes. It was remarkable; one of the finest examples of boat handling I have ever seen. The spinnaker, gollywobbler and all the rest came down without a hitch which was just as well as there was very little room to manoeuvre between the finishing line and the harbour wall. We then motored into the harbour to run the gauntlet of the customary water fights with hoses and water bombs, plastic bags filled with water, thrown at each boat by crews on other boats.

Aboard Altair on the starting line

This is how the youthful crews let off steam before the nightly festivities. I had been given a ticket to the reception at the yacht club for owners and crews by the skipper of *Cintra* as he preferred to go on a pub crawl, so I duly turned up to find some very well known people there. I saw Elizabeth Meyer the owner of *Endeavour* on the other side of the room and asked a friend to introduce me. I told her I once had a Nicholson boat (the 8 Metre *Wye*) which was built in the same yard as *Endeavour* and was known by the men in the yard as the "Little Endeavour" due to her long overhanging Nicholson bow. She was very pleasant and we had an interesting chat. Elizabeth

Meyer has since been involved with the revival of the "J" Class which no-one could have anticipated a few years ago. A day to remember indeed!

On the Friday it blew hard and racing for the smaller boats was cancelled. *Altair* and *Adix* made a spectacular sight as they had their own private duel. There was also an historic contest between old and modern America's Cup challengers. *Endeavour* and *Ville de Paris* battled it out in a match race to establish how fast the modern America's Cup Class design was compared to the 58 year old "J" class boat. Many assumed the result would be a foregone conclusion in favour of the new design but upwind *Endeavour* had a significant lead. Downwind, *Endeavour* with a crew of 50 on board set her 13,455 square foot spinnaker, nicknamed the "planetarium" as it is blue and white covered with stars but the lighter, smaller *Ville de Paris* pulled ahead and beat her to the finish. It was a spectacular sight and I had a good view of the start and finish along with the huge crowd on the harbour wall.

During the week I explored the neighbouring marina where the smaller yachts were berthed. There I found the 6 and 8 Metres and was excited to find *Christina* re-named with her original name *Ilderim* and owned by Marc Buschotts from Belgium. I spent a pleasant evening with him and his crew comparing our activities of 30 years before with the changed scene of the 90's. I saw a beautiful 8 that seemed familiar and to my surprise discovered it was Fries Ballantines old 1927 Anker and Jensen designed *Margaret* under French ownership. I recognised her stern but could not see the name until I spoke to a crew member who invited me aboard. I was certain when I found the Royal Clyde Yacht Club Centenary Cruise plaque on the bulkhead. *Margaret* had been completely re-built and was in excellent condition with new Kevlar sails. To my surprise she won the 8 Metre class for the week as on the Clyde she had never raced in the class and was not generally rated. The gaff rigged *Esteril* also did well and the contrast of design compared to newer eights was very interesting. Another surprise was that the unsuccessful British America's Cup challenger *Sovereign* won in the 12 Metre class in competition with the famous and supposedly faster *Vim, Flica II* and *Tomahawk*.

In 1998 I took part in the Maritime Festival at Brest in Brittany. This was an amazing event with over 2,500 traditional sailing boats, large and small attending from all over the world. I was a guest aboard *Madcap* the oldest Bristol Channel Pilot Cutter afloat, built in 1875 and owned by Adrian Spence from Belfast who I had got to know at Portaferry a few years before when we took part in *Macaria*. There were a few funny moments and the Irishmen seemed more interested in drinking Guinness in the Irish pub (at inflated prices) than sailing. The event was spectacular, attracting over one million visitors and the weather was good. Many French fishing ports had built replicas of their particular type of traditional sailing fishing boats for the event and the fleet included everything from tall ships, classic yachts, pilot cutters, English oyster smacks, French Tunnymen, schooners, ketches, yawls and cutters of all sizes. I even had a sail aboard an 18 foot long home built gaff schooner, complete with topsails and fisherman's staysail. This boat was trailed by road from Ireland for the week. I also saw the old pilot cutter *Leonora* now under her original name *Marie Fernand* and based at her original home port of Le Havre.

Wednesday 17th July was a momentous one in the history of sail. I cannot imagine any previous event where so many sailing vessels were concentrated in one place at one time. At least 30 were over 100 feet long and the horizon was completely filled with sails as far as the eye could see. It was impossible to take it all in at once, far less identify many. Some of the more notable vessels were the three mast barques *Europa* and *Stadsraad Lehmkuhl,* topsail schooners *Pride of Baltimore* and *Ostershelde* and historic replicas such as *Matthew* along with French fishing boats, Thames and Dutch sailing barges along with almost every other type of traditional sailing boat imaginable. This event is held every four years followed by the fleet sailing to Douarnenez where the festival continues.

Madcap was tied up near the aforementioned Irish pub and the crew found it too convenient. I met *Johnny Hellion* in his Galway Hooker *Morning Star* in another part of the vast harbour. He had chartered his boat to Guinness and took visitors sailing where they could drink as much Guinness as they wanted for free! Needless to say there were a few long faces aboard *Madcap* as some of them had spent all their money on overpriced Guinness ashore

Boats at Brest 1998

In 2001 the America's Cup Jubilee Regatta was held at Cowes. This was an awesome event with over 200 yachts celebrating the 150th anniversary of the schooner *America's* challenge for the ornate Victorian silver jug named after the first challenger as the famous *America's Cup*. I will not try and document the history of the subsequent challenges here as several books have been written on the subject but many attempts were made by Great Britain to take the cup from the Americans which Australia finally achieved in 1983. The first competitors were large gaff cutters followed by the American "J" class rule boats in the thirties. British challengers included Sir Thomas Lipton's five different *Shamrocks* and Tom Sopwith's *Endeavours I and II*. The America's Cup had been dormant since the war but the rules were changed from the previous J Class boats to the more modest 12 Metre Class. In 1958 Great Britain challenged for the cup and *Sceptre* designed by David Boyd and built at Robertson's at Sandbank on the Clyde was selected as the challenging boat. The series was a disaster for Britain and *Sceptre* but I do not think the boat was as bad as many thought. There is no doubt that the Americans had much more experience and resources at the time. Other challengers were built and in the eighties there were many new twelves built in the U.S.A., Great Britain, Australia, France, Italy and New Zealand specifically for the America's Cup.

An amazing 37 Twelve Metre Class yachts were entered for the Cowes regatta including former America's Cup winners *Columbia, Intrepid, Freedom, Australia II, America and New Zealand* along with many former challengers and would be challengers of the past. Impressive as the twelves were, the real stars of the show were the three "J" class yachts, *Endeavour I, Shamrock V, Velsheda* and the beautifully restored Fife 23 Metre *Cambria* racing with them. The replica of the original schooner *America* was also there along with an amazing collection of large and small classic boats from 11 different countries. There were also many modern yachts, including the 82 foot all black *Stealth* owned by Fiat boss Gianni Agnelli, the spectacular *Maria Chia III* and five new modern America's cup class yachts.

I sailed with my old German friends in *Senta* who had come over from Bremen for the regatta. It was good to see the brothers and their families again and to sail in the old lady. *Senta* had been very well maintained and was in excellent condition. We took part in the Round the Island race on the Tuesday when the "J's" and other racing boats disappeared over the horizon leaving us with a number of others fighting a foul tide at St. Catherine's Point. The weather was generally good, although on some days there was too much wind. The main attraction though was simply to see this great fleet of yachts, a pageant of yachting history. The "J's" and other large yachts were moored off the Royal Yacht Squadron and the others were crammed into the marinas with extra pontoons provided for the week. The organisation was fantastic with free water taxis at your beck and call day and night. Just to sit on deck and watch the passing traffic, one beautiful boat after another heading up or down the Medina River was a rare treat.

Although we had not seen large classic yachts in Scotland for many years except for the occasional visitor, this was all to change with the advent of the Fife Regatta in 1998. Alastair Houston the marine artist and his sister Fiona organised a special regatta for Fife yachts and invited every known owner of these boats from many countries to a week long event on the Clyde. A small but impressive fleet of Fife boats assembled at Largs Marina. These included *Moonbeam,* the 67 ton gaff cutter now known as *Moonbeam of Fife,* not to be confused with the larger 93 ton 95ft *Moonbeam* which was not at this event. The recently restored 1923 87 ton gaff ketch *Kentra, Magda IV* from Sweden, *Pen Duick* from Brittany, *Solway Maid, Elise, Madrigal* and *Starlight* with *Mignon* and *Vagrant* as the only local boats. Although just a small number of the Fife yachts that could have attended, it was wonderful to see them all gathered at Largs near their place of birth at Fairlie. Unfortunately the week started on a very sad note. Eric Tabarly was lost overboard from his yacht *Pen Duick* in the Irish Sea on passage to the Clyde. Apparently he went forward at night to douse the mainsail in a squall without a safety harness and was knocked overboard by the gaff. The crew looked for him all night in strong winds and steep seas but could not find him in the dark. Even in June the water temperature was only 11 degrees Celsius and no one could have survived for long in such conditions. His body was recovered five weeks later by French fishermen in the Irish Sea. In spite of the tragedy the crew continued their passage to the Clyde but did not race. Eric's wife Jacqueline and two daughters arrived and the French ensign flew at half mast on *Pen Duick* all week. Eric Tabarly was much loved and respected in France where sailing has a much higher profile and greater public interest than in this country. He had won many races in six different yachts all called *Pen Duick*, including the Fastnet Race in 1967 and broke records in the Ostar, Whitbread, San Francisco to Tokyo and other major events. He was one of the greatest yachtsmen of our time but of all his *Pen Duick's*, his 100 year old Fife was his favourite and when he was at home she was moored in front of his house at Benodet in Brittany. He once ordered new mainsheet blocks for *Pen Duick* from my Classic Marine business. His cheque was accompanied by a personal letter which I thought was a really nice and unusual gesture.

    This first Fife regatta was a success although the weather was very mixed. I sailed on *Solway Maid* in the race from Hunter's Quay to Rothesay in breezy conditions with rain showers. *Moonbeam* was first home by a big margin and in the evening we were entertained at a reception at Mount Stuart the magnificent family home of the Marquis of Bute. At the reception I met Don Street the very experienced American cruising man who with his yacht *Iolaire* is well known in the Caribbean and other parts of the world. He told me he was short handed for his forthcoming passage to Sweden and asked me if I would care to join him. I declined for business and family reasons. Alastair and Fiona did a first class job in organising the regatta and promised to hold a larger event a few years later.

    True to their word the next Fife Regatta took place in June 2003. This was a much bigger event and a total of 23 boats came from several countries. The largest Fife yacht this time was the 93 ton *Moonbeam* although there were some even larger yachts present, but not racing as they were not designed by Fife; more of this later. The regatta entries are shown below:

Name	Rig	Length	Year
Belle Adventure	Bermudan Ketch	93' 9"	1929
Clio	Bermudan Sloop	45' 9"	1921
Hatasoo	Gaff Sloop 17/19 class	19'	1894
Jap	Gaff sloop Cork O.D.	36' 7"	1897
Kentra	Gaff Ketch	85'	1923
Kookaburra	M.S.O.D Sloop	24' 6"	1929
Lotus	Bermudan Sloop	24'	1897
Mignon	Bermudan Sloop	28'	1898
Mikado	Clyde 30 Bmdn Cutter	42'	1899
Moonbeam	Gaff Cutter	105'	1914
Pierette	Gaff Sloop	27' 3"	1899
Rosemary	Bermudan Sloop	38' 6"	1925
Seabird	Gaff Cutter	28'	2002
Sian II	M.S.O.D Sloop	24' 6"	1929
Siglen	M.S.O.D Sloop	24' 6"	1927
Solway Maid	Bermudan Cutter	52'	1937
Sonata	Bermudan Sloop	51' 5"	1950
Sunshine	Int. 6 Metre Sloop	35' 6"	1927
Tern	Belfast Lough O.D.	37' 3"	1897
The Lady Anne	Int.15 Metre Cutter	72'	1912
Thelma 3	M.S.O.D Sloop	24' 6"	1899
Viola	Gaff Cutter	49'	1908

In addition to the Fife yachts the majestic three masted schooners *Adix* and *Shenandoah* attended. Anchored off the marina their presence really "put the icing on the cake".

The newest boat was *Seabird* built in France in wood epoxy to a Fife design of 1889. This boat has attracted interest from many places and three have been built so far. *Seabird* was an interesting contrast to *Hatasoo* the 17/19 class boat of 1894, the smallest and oldest Fife yacht present, still based on the Clyde winning her class sailed by her owners the McGrouther brothers from Kilcreggan. *Hatasoo* was a revolutionary boat in her day and her underwater shape is remarkably modern. She was so fast that the other 17/19 boats could not compete, leading to the demise of the class.

Hattasoo

I was particularly interested in the wonderful 15 Metre *The Lady Anne* which had been completely rebuilt at Fairlie Restorations on the Hamble. It is said that the only original parts of the boat are the lead keel and the bronze mainsheet bollards! Whether considered a new boat or a restoration, she has been faithfully fitted out with such attention to detail that she is exactly as originally built. An exception is that her topmast is built in carbon fibre sheathed in wood which seems to me to be an excellent idea. These big cutters often lost their topmasts when racing and the other 15 Metre *Tuiga* has broken hers at least once in recent times. Unfortunately *The Lady Anne* is not allowed to race with *Tuiga* in the Mediterranean, but is forced to compete in the "Spirit of Tradition" class due to the organisers' purist views on this innovation. I managed to get an opportunity to sail on her at Largs. This was the day before the first race and with Paul Goss, who also skippers the schooner *Adix* at the helm; we stormed up and down the Largs Channel in a force 5 in company with *Moonbeam*. It was an exhilarating experience and an eye opener for some of the visitors aboard who had never sailed on a large classic yacht before. *The Lady Anne* has no winches of any type and sheets and backstays are all tensioned with tackles. Due to the size and power of the rig the running backstays are critical and when tacking and gybing great care must be taken. As on previous occasions in *Altair* and *Cintra*, I was impressed by the skill and professionalism of the skipper and crew.

We watched the first race which was round the Great Cumbrae from my little Oysterman *Ruach*. The weather was sunny with light winds and the sight of these magnificent yachts gliding along in light airs with the hazy sun shining through their sails was never to be forgotten. In the evening at the crews' party at Kelburn Estate, Paul Goss offered me a berth aboard *Adix* for the passage to Rhu the following day. Although *Adix* was not officially in the race she was allowed to sail along with the fleet. *Adix* is a magnificent vessel. Originally built in Spain as *Jessica* in 1984 for an Argentinean businessman, she was then bought by the Australian entrepreneur Alan Bond who renamed her *Schooner XXXX*. She was sold again to her present Spanish owner and considerably altered and improved in 1992 at Pendennis Shipyard at Falmouth. Paul Goss has been her captain since that time and managed the project. He had previously managed the restoration of both *Altair* and *Belle Aventure* (ex *Eileen*) and is one of the world's most experienced classic yacht skippers. *Adix* is 174 feet overall with a modest beam of 23 feet and her displacement weight is 370 tons. She combines the best of traditional gaff rig with modern technology, for example the masts are aluminium and other spars wood, reinforced with carbon fibre. The gaff sails hoist on tracks rather than the more traditional hoops. Topsails are also set on tracks from the deck with no need for crew to go aloft as in other large schooners. The sail area is 13,800 square feet, increasing to 28,000 square feet downwind with the addition of gollywobblers and spinnaker. Some of the halyards are of Spectra with conventional rope tails for ease of hoisting and there are power winches enabling the ship to be sailed with a small deck crew of only 6 although there is a permanent professional crew of 14. In 2002 *Adix* along with another schooner *Windrose* beat the record set for the passage from New York to the Lizard by the three mast schooner *Atlantic* in 1905. The passage was made in 11 days and 10 hours, averaging 11 knots and breaking the *Atlantic's* record of 12 days and 4 hours which had never previously been beaten by a monohull sailing vessel although Eric Tabarly broke the record in the trimaran *Paul Ricard* in 1980. A spectacular vessel indeed, just to go aboard and see the acres of teak deck and the wonderful workmanship of the fittings, hatches and deckhouses and size of the gear is an experience in itself but I was actually going to sail on her. I could hardly sleep the night before!

Adix at Largs 2003 (photo by Neil MacGregor)

On arriving at the marina I went aboard *Adix* and was introduced to various crew members. They were an international bunch and mostly in their twenties. There were several Australians; Paul Goss is from Tasmania and one girl from Eastern Europe. We got underway and set all sail; foresail, mainsail and mizzen with their topsails and three headsails. The wind was northerly, force 3 to 4 which promised a windward beat up the Firth. Paul at the helm let the Fife fleet get away and then we hardened our sheets and sailed close hauled towards Toward Lighthouse on the Cowal shore. The sheer power of the ship was soon evident as she sailed beautifully to windward. Her gaff rig with jib headed topsails formed a perfect curve, as clean as a modern bermuda rig. *Adix* pointed well, tacking through about 85 degrees. To my surprise and delight Paul offered me the helm and I spent the afternoon steering this magnificent vessel up the Firth. We had a wonderful view of the racing boats and *The Lady Anne* soon took the lead, pointing as high as a modern yacht and looking magnificent. There were many boats surrounding us, Yachts, power boats, R.I.B.s and the paddle steamer *Waverley*. Some boats came very close and from one I heard someone calling my name. I looked down to the boat below and a female voice said "It's Gordon!" I hadn't a clue who she was, as I was trying to concentrate on sailing the ship and the lady had an oilskin hood covering half her face so I just smiled and waved. I discovered later that she was Lesley Main from Arran who was there with her brother Michael to see the fleet. Apparently she told the others in the boat that I was the owner!!! Many other boats came close on our way up the river and as we arrived at the finishing line off the Cloch lighthouse which was provided by Brian Young in *Glenafton,* who greeted us with a gun after *The Lady Anne* had finished first. In return we fired a salute from our bronze cannon which sat on the after deck.

I had the opportunity to talk to Adix's owner during the afternoon and he was interested to hear about the history of Clyde yachting. I pointed out the places where *The Lady Anne* had raced 90 years before – Hunter's Quay, Gourock, and Kilcreggan. I also mentioned that 2003 was the centenary of the Royal Gourock Yacht Club and he suggested we sail in close to greet the members. Paul called up *The Lady Anne* on the V.H.F. and told them to sail straight into the anchorage. We followed and both yachts sailed right up to the club moorings and as we tacked out again fired our cannons. It must have looked wonderful from the shore but I am sure some of the locals thought they were being attacked by pirates! Unfortunately there were not many people at the club at the time, but our salute was gratefully acknowledged. We then beat up to the Gareloch where we anchored *Adix* under sail in Rosneath Bay. Paul always tries to manoeuvre *Adix* under sail whenever possible and it was impressive to see how he had everything quietly under control. The owner was anxious to go ashore with his wife for his daily walk and Paul landed them ashore at Rosneath while most of the crew went over to Rhu where the other boats had gathered at the Marina.

Two days later I, along with my brother Kenneth took the ferry to Rothesay to join the *Adix* again, this time for the race from Tighnabruaich to Largs. It was another lovely day and as we arrived at Rothesay the sight of the yachts anchored in the bay dominated by *Adix, Shenandoah* and *Moonbeam,* was just like a painting or photo of 100 years earlier. We got out to the ship and found the crew getting everything ready. All sail was set and we got underway without any fuss. There were several new guests aboard including Duncan Walker of Fairlie Restorations and we made our way up the Kyles of Bute with the rest of the fleet through the Narrows to the start at Tighnabruaich. There was a pleasant south westerly breeze and the many spectator boats were dodging the yachts before the start. It was an excellent day for photographers and some wonderful shots were taken and later included in the Fife Regatta calendar of 2004. The race eventually started and as we were not racing, we waited until the fleet got away then followed, overtaking most of them before the island of Inchmarnock.

The wind gradually died away which did not deter *The Lady Anne* as she worked her way to windward far ahead of the rest of the fleet. She had been leading most of the week and *Moonbeam* was unable to catch her although she is the larger yacht. We watched and cheered as *The Lady Anne* crossed the finishing line coming alongside us after we anchored. *Adix* then hosted a party on deck for all the crews, when the dinghy was turned into a gigantic ice bucket to cool the beer and wine. It was good to meet owners and crews from all the yachts and much good humoured banter was exchanged. Guided tours of *Adix* were laid on and everyone was impressed by the comfort and quality below. Even the crew's quarters are luxurious! The all stainless steel galley is set on gimbals and there is a walk-in freezer. We did not have access to the owner's quarters but we did see the saloon and dining room which has beautiful panelling with a cleverly concealed T.V. The ship is self sufficient for many days with vast stowage space, a water maker and the latest technology with satellite communications systems allowing the owner to conduct his business aboard anywhere in the world. We all came back on deck amazed by what we had seen.

Paul Goss at the helm of Adix with the Lady Anne in the background

This was the end of the regatta, the yachts gradually left for home. Some cruised on the west coast for a few weeks and I saw *Kentra* at Oban a few weeks later. It seems the visitors really enjoyed themselves and were impressed by the hospitality, the scenery, the organisation and even the weather which had been very kind and showed off Scotland at her best. Alastair and Fiona Houston ably assisted by Carolyn Elder of Largs Yacht Haven did a wonderful job again and we are all looking forward to an even bigger event the next time.

These are just a few of the highlights of my experiences in classic yachts. Interest in these boats continues to grow around the world and several other famous yachts have been, or are currently being restored. These include the 186 ton cutter *Lulworth*, The Nicholson 107 ton cutter *Merrymaid,* The Gruber designed German yawl *Nordwind* and the Fife 19 Metre *Mariquita*. New builds include replicas of the royal yacht *Britannia* and the famous racing schooner *Westward* named *Elenora*. The "J" class is flourishing again with Elizabeth Meyer as a prime mover and a replica of the famous America's Cup Defender *Ranger* has now joined the fleet. Although all this activity is going on we see little of it here in Scotland. There are many traditional boats on the English east coast and the West Country and Ireland also have significant numbers. Sadly though there are very few classic boats in Scotland. This is strange when one reflects on the fact that some of the world's finest yacht designers and builders of the past were from the West of Scotland. Three generations of William Fifes, G. L. Watson, Alfred Milne, James McGruer and David Boyd left their marks on the yachting scene out of all proportion to the size of their country, just as the Clyde shipyards dominated shipbuilding in the early years of the 20th century. Mirroring the decline of shipbuilding on the Clyde, there are practically no yacht yards left now. Robertsons, Morris & Lorimers, Fairlie Yacht Slip, McGruers, Adams, McLean's and others have all disappeared and Silvers of Rosneath and Sandpoint at Dumbarton, (formerly McAllister's) remain as practically the sole remaining yards. At the time of writing John Hill at Clyde River Boatyard is due to close due to a major housing development on the site at Renfrew. G. L. Watson and McGruer's survive as consultancy and design businesses but actual boat building on the Clyde hardly exists now.

To conclude the chapter on a more optimistic note it is encouraging to see what is happening elsewhere and perhaps the classic boat revival will eventually come to Scotland. There are a few local events such as the Tarbert Traditional Boat Festival, The McGruer Classic Regatta and the Clyde Corinthian Yacht Club's events but interest will only grow if enthusiasts take part and actively promote their interest.

Adix on the wind

Chapter 8 - Tall Ships

Ever since I was a small boy I have been fascinated by large sailing ships. I used to collect postcards and pictures from magazines and remember my excitement when my father took me to see the American Coastguard barque *Eagle* when she visited Glasgow in the fifties. I was too young to see the last of the working sailers at Kingston Dock where they usually berthed but sailing ships captivated me and I was determined to sail on one someday. My mother used to tell me to stop dreaming about ships of the past but I could only think of how I would love to have made a voyage in one of the great Erikson vessels following in the footsteps of Eric Newby, Alan Villiers and others who had written of their experiences in the books I devoured. I collected and read many books. Lubbock, Underhill, Villiers and others fuelled my interest and I dreamed that someday my opportunity would come. Gustav Erikson was a Finnish ship owner who bought a number of large sailing vessels cheaply after the great depression. By 1938 he owned the largest fleet of square rigged vessels in the world at the time. By purchasing the ships for scrap value and using them for cargos which did not have to be delivered by a specific time such as grain from Australia and nitrates from South America, he was able to make them pay until the war changed everything. In the 1930's many young people were able to sign on as crew members in these ships. Eric Newby's excellent book "The Last Grain Race" tells his story of a voyage in the *Moshulu* a 3,200 ton Clyde built four masted barque now a museum ship in America. This was of course all in the past and as a young boy I could not see how it would ever be possible to sail in such ships but life is full of surprises and events gradually unfolded which would make my dream come true.

In 1956 the first race for large sailing ships was organised by the newly formed Sail Training Association. This was the first time since the war that a number of large sailing vessels had gathered and probably the first organised race for sailing ships. The famous grain and tea clipper races of the past were not organised events but simply different ships racing to be first home with their cargos. The course for the race was from Torbay to Lisbon and entrants included the three mast schooner *Creole,* the three mast barques *Sagres* from Portugal and *Galatea* from Spain, now in Glasgow with her original name *Glenlee* along with various smaller vessels. It is interesting to reflect on the remarks made by Alan Villiers at that time reporting on the event, when he said pessimistically it was probably the last opportunity to see such ships and unlikely that such an event would be possible in the future. He did not foresee the amazing growth in sailing ships which took place in the following decades. Although not my favourite expression, the term "Tall Ship" is commonly used today to describe a square rigged vessel or windjammer as they are sometimes called. This is a relatively new description and originates from John Masefield's poem, Sea Fever *"I must down to the seas again, to the lonely sea and the sky, And all I ask is a tall ship and a star to steer her by"* The sail training races became known as the "Tall Ships Races" the name stuck and nowadays everyone, sailors or non sailors alike understand what is meant by a "Tall Ship".

Although the Tall Ships Race had become a regular event, I did not foresee as a schoolboy how I could sail on one of these ships, as the crews seemed to be all naval or merchant navy cadets. In the early sixties I was excited to hear that the Sail Training Association was to build a ship for Britain. Sailing ships of other nationalities were well known. Norway had the *Christian Radich, Sorlandet* and *Statsraad Lehmkuhl*. Denmark had the *Danmark* and *Georg Stage*. Germany had the *Gorch Fock* and there were others. The new ship was to be a three masted schooner designed by Camper and Nicholson and built at Dunston's shipyard at Hessle near Hull. Bill Strang, the commodore of the Clyde Cruising Club at the time was a member of the local S.T.A. committee. He was friendly with my father and knowing of my interest told me how to apply as crew for the maiden voyage. The schooner was named *Sir Winston Churchill* and launched after a delay of six months, due to an accident when the ship fell over in her building berth part completed. This was rectified with no further problems but everything was delayed resulting in frantic activity to be ready for the maiden voyage in April 1966. The *Sir Winston Churchill* was a steel topsail schooner with gaff fore and mainsails and bermudan mizzen, with a square topsail on the foremast setting a raffee above. The rig was designed to be easily handled by a small crew but with enough work for 36 trainees. Her vital statistics were L.O.A. 135 feet Beam 25 feet, Sail Area 7,110 square feet. (compare this with *Adix* in the previous chapter) The permanent crew consisted of captain, first mate, bosun, engineer and cook assisted by unpaid bosun's mate and cook's assistant. A volunteer purser, navigator, three watch officers and three watch leaders were chosen from experienced yachtsmen who applied but these usually changed on each voyage. I had been offered the position of watch leader which I felt was a great honour.

I joined the *Sir Winston Churchill* at Hull where I met the captain Glynn Griffiths and first mate Mike Webb, along with the other watch leaders and watch officers. There were three watches, fore, main and mizzen and I was put in charge of the main watch trainees under my watch officer Brian Stewart. Brian was a very experienced yachtsman and Lloyd's underwriter. He owned *Zulu* a Laurent Giles 19 tonner built by Morris and Lorimer in 1957 (now named *Cetewago.)* Due to the delays at the yard there was no time for proper sea trials and we left Hull with many jobs to do. I soon got into the way of being a watch leader and learned how to organise my watch of twelve boys. Most had never been to sea before and it was very instructive seeing how some changed from aggressive, somewhat fearful individuals into confident, useful deck hands in only two weeks.

We were all new to this and even the captain had no previous experience of handling such a ship. On leaving Hull docks for the first time we had to turn the ship through 180 degrees and as her head came round in the narrow dock the wind caught her and the bowsprit scraped against the dock wall removing a slice of wood from the end plug. I believe the mark remains to this day but fortunately no real damage was done. We were due to dock in Portsmouth the home port the following week and the sailing trials were successful with enough wind to try out all the sails and gear but not too much for an inexperienced crew. We were accompanied by press boats and helicopters, photographing and filming us for newspapers and T.V. Bruce Banks the sailmaker was aboard making adjustments as we sailed south and many small jobs were done by all the crew. I spent a few happy hours making the net under the bowsprit with Chris the bosun and the weather was kind to us. Once we entered the Channel the Captain felt a run ashore would be good for the boys so we anchored at Dover for a night to carry on the next day to Portsmouth.

After sorting out our teething troubles all hands had much more confidence in the ship and pleased with the way she handled. So much so, that Glynn decided that when we arrived in Portsmouth harbour, we would try to berth under sail, weather permitting. This seemed a bold move and we rehearsed our plan, until everyone had a clear idea of their duties. On arriving with what seemed like most of the world's media watching us, we had a light wind on the beam making our entrance to the harbour relatively easy. Glynn giving the helm orders, guided us slowly in under reduced sail and we gently came alongside in the naval dockyard near the Royal yacht *Britannia*, dropping the remaining sails in a perfect manoeuvre with trainees manning the topsail yards. There was a great cheer from the crowd and in the evening the crew were all invited to a mayor's reception at the Town Hall. We were all plagued by reporters and photographers and many of us, were interviewed. It was certainly a fine beginning for the S.T.A.'s first vessel.

One year later Sir James Miller, who had the distinction of having been both the Lord Provost of Edinburgh and the Lord Mayor of London, lost his son Malcolm in a car accident. He offered to donate a sum of £75,000 towards the cost of another ship, on condition that she was to be named after his son and built in Scotland. The new vessel was to be an identical sister ship to the *Churchill* and the John Lewis shipyard in Aberdeen won the contract. Sir James Miller's generous gift paid a large proportion of the cost of the ship but extra funds were required. Money was raised by local volunteer committees in various towns round the British Isles and my father became chairman of the Glasgow and West of Scotland committee. We held various fund raising events and received all sorts of donations in cash and kind from many sources. Once the new *Malcolm Miller* was completed, she was christened by Lady Miller and once again I had the opportunity to sail on her short maiden voyage. This time due to my previous experience I was made watch officer and had more responsibility. The first captain of the *Malcolm Miller* was Mike Willoughby who had previous experience in square rig and was a fund of knowledge. The ship had a few improvements from the *Churchill* but was essentially the same. It was difficult to tell them apart form a distance but one clue was that the *Churchill* had rounded tops to the deckhouse doors and the *Miller's* were square.

Sir Winston Churchill on sailing trials

I made another voyage to the south coast of Ireland in the *Miller* as watch officer again, where we met some of my old friends in Cork. Somehow I never got round to sailing in either the *Churchill* or *Miller* after that time. The two schooners did a fine job over 35 years but by the Millennium the S.T.A. eventually decided to replace them, as maintenance and repair costs were becoming a major problem. The ships had been well used every year with an amazing number of miles on their logs. Both ships were to be sold and replaced by two new vessels rigged as brigs. The *Stavros Niarchos* and the *Prince William* would operate in the same tried and tested way as the previous ships, but with more trainees. As the rig is more complicated and entails more going aloft than in the schooners, they are in my opinion more interesting to sail and provide better hands-on experience.

The S.T.A. has given over 60,000 young men and women (and also older people) the opportunity of a lifetime, to do something completely different from their everyday life. People of very different backgrounds experience living and working together, in sometimes uncomfortable and possibly frightening conditions, often in bad weather. They come to know that their actions affect everyone else aboard the ship and above all they get to know themselves. They come to understand what they are capable of in situations that would rarely be possible ashore. I believe this is one of the most valuable lessons we can give young people. I have seen streetwise troublemakers completely transformed during their voyage. The quiet ones come alive and gain confidence and the difficult ones usually change for the better. Of course it may not last when they come home again but I am sure that the experience will affect them for the rest of their lives. If this country operated a fleet of large sailing ships, with all young people having to spend a few weeks at sea, I wonder if there would be so much trouble in our towns and city streets.

Shipmates

One amusing experience aboard the *Churchill* comes to mind. Many of the trainees are seasick, as even if they are not prone to seasickness, the sight and sound of others is enough to make anyone sick! One day I was on watch on the bridge with a young trainee on the wheel. He was looking a bit green and as everyone knows, it helps to concentrate on steering. After about half an hour he turned to me and said "Could you please take the wheel for a moment sir?" He then leaned over the side of the bridge for a few minutes, came back to the wheel and cheerfully said "Just a quick one sir!"

In 1966 Brian Stewart asked me to crew with him in his yacht *Zulu* in the Tall Ship's race from Falmouth to Copenhagen. *Zulu* was in class C which was for the smallest vessels. The rules state that majority of the crew have to be below 25 years old and we had several medical students making up the crew. David Revel who had been a fellow watch leader with me on the *Churchill's* maiden voyage was also in the crew. The other boys were great fun but hygiene was not their strong point, I had never expected medical students to be so messy!

From the bowsprit – Sir Winston Churchill

After the start at Falmouth, we had a wonderful spinnaker run in sunshine most of the way up the English Channel and across the North Sea to the Skaw where the race finished. It was great to be racing in company with square riggers and other large vessels and as we were well up in the fleet we had high hopes of a prize. We did indeed win a prize – first in our class and celebrations were the order of the day. Our main rival was the Lloyd's Yacht Club boat *Lutine*. We heard later that back in London, Lloyds had thought that *Lutine* had won the race and the famous Lutine Bell was rung twice in her honour. The bell is only rung with a single strike when a ship is reported lost and more than once to announce a special event. The officials were spared any embarrassment for their mistake however by the fact that Brian Stewart with *Zulu* was also a member of Lloyds. We met with other ship's crews and the Norwegian full rigged ship *Sorlandet* was moored nearby and Brian and her captain agreed to exchange some crew for the short passage to Copenhagen. I was given the opportunity to sail on the *Sorlandet* and went aboard to meet the huge crew of young Norwegian boys. My brother Kenneth had raced to Copenhagen in the *Statsraad Lehmkuhl* which is a large three mast barque also from Norway, so I was keen to sail in a real square rigger too; my childhood dream came true at last! We had an uneventful passage to Copenhagen for a couple of days but for me it was wonderful. We worked on the yards setting and furling sails on watch or cleaned the ship during the day and slept in hammocks off watch. Most of the Norwegian trainees spoke a little English so communication was not a problem. I was delighted to be given the wheel for an hour and found myself chatting to the captain which one is not supposed to do when steering! In my defence he spoke to me first.

On arriving at Copenhagen we anchored near the other large vessels and spent a few days relaxing, looking round the town and visiting other ships. The *Sir Winston Churchill* had just taken part in her first race and I met up with her permanent crew who had become good friends. One night we took the *Churchill's* lifeboat and cruised along the canals. Copenhagen is like Amsterdam in that there is a network of canals through the city. We were making a lot of noise and attracted attention from passers-by, when on going under a bridge we got stuck. The boat was just too big or to put it another way the bridge was too low! Our exuberance cooled down when we thought we had a major problem as we had taken the lifeboat without permission. Just as we were expecting the long arm of the Danish law or the wrath of the captain, a final shove freed the boat and we slowly returned and tied the boat up hoping we had not been seen. We got away with it and at the end of the week everyone took part in the customary parade through the city, when each ship's crew marches to the prizegiving to the sound of a brass band, the naval crews in their smart uniforms and others in matching shirts or jerseys. The *Zulu* crew were proud indeed to see our skipper Brian go forward to receive the cup; a grand finale to a wonderful week. Brian invited me to sail in *Zulu* again and I joined him for the Fastnet race in 1968.

Just as the interest in classic yachts has grown in recent years there has been similar growth of interest in large sailing ships. Since the break up of the Soviet Union, several Russian and Eastern European ships can be seen in western waters. There are a number of important vessels in these countries and Russia owns the two four masted barques *Kruzenstern* and *Sedov* in their fleet. Both ships are real Cape Horners; they were built at the end of the sailing ship era for German owners. The *Sedov* formerly *Magdalene Vinnen* later *Kommodore Johnsen* is 385 feet overall and 3,476 tons gross and the *Kruzenstern,* formerly *Padua* is 375 feet overall and 3,545 tons gross. These are two of the largest sailing vessels afloat and historically very important. Today most Russian ships train cadets for the Russian merchant navy and fishing fleets and they are regular participants in Tall Ships Races. Other nations' ships are too numerous to mention in detail here but it is exciting to note that since the bold step by the S.T.A. of building the schooners almost 40 years ago, several new square riggers have been built in Britain since that time. These are the brig *Royalist,* the three mast barques *Lord Nelson* and *Tenacious* and the two new brigs which replaced the S.T.A. schooners *Stavros Niarchos* and *Prince William*. I would also like to mention two new vessels which are particular favourites of mine; the *Stad Amsterdam* from the Netherlands and the *Cisne Branca* from Brazil. These are identical three masted full rigged ships built in Holland on the lines of the 19th century tea clippers. They are beautiful and fast and the *Stad Amsterdam* has been successful in several races. The list in the appendix shows a selection of the world's principal vessels at the time of writing. Note how many are of relatively recent build.

In 1997 I heard about "Tall Ship Friends", a German based organisation that organises voyages for paying guests or trainees as they are called, on a variety of ships of different nationalities. It is a non-profit organisation and the objective is to help safeguard the future of the fleet of sailing vessels owned by the former U.S.S.R. countries formerly financed by the Russian and Baltic State governments. All the money from voyage fees is used to help maintain and equip these ships and Tall Ship Friends recently purchased the three mast barque *Tovarisch* formerly the German navy's *Gorch Fock 1*. She is currently being restored and refitted in Hamburg and will sail again under her original name. I contacted Joan O'Neil at the U.K. office and decided to apply for a berth on the Russian ship *Mir* for the Tall Ships race from Aberdeen to Trondheim in Norway. I was pleased to get a berth and on arriving in Aberdeen found the usual crowds on the dockside and sailing vessels in every corner of the harbour. If you have never attended a Tall Ships Race, it is an experience not to be missed. Some of the world's largest and finest sailing vessels attend and square rigged ships, barques, brigs, schooners, and many smaller yachts crowd the port. Wherever the race is held, thousands of spectators visit the ships and line the shore to watch them sailing away. People are fascinated by large sailing ships and the host ports compete fiercely for the honour. Scotland has hosted the Tall Ships Races more often than most countries. Aberdeen, Greenock and Leith have all held the event more than once in recent times. The atmosphere is amazing with young people, music and food of many nationalities. Regular attendees include British, Russian, Polish, Italian, French, German, Norwegian, Danish, Swedish, U.S.A., South American and even Mexican crews.

I soon found the *Mir* (peace in Russian) and was immediately impressed. She is a three mast ship and one of six identical sisters. These are the *Dar Mlojesy* (Poland), the *Kershones* (Ukraine) and three other Russian ships *Druzhba, Naziezda* and *Pallada* . They are all of recent build by the Gdask Shipyard in Poland and are rigged as modern three masted full rigged ships. Their overall length is 310 feet with flush decks from forward to aft with no poop, forecastle or bulwarks. This would have raised the eyebrows of some of the old Cape Horn sailors! The ships are certainly fast and the *Mir* has the reputation as the fastest square rigger afloat. There are several novel features in the rig; for example all the yards are fixed without topsail, topgallant or royal halyards. This simplifies the running rigging and reduces windage, but can make clewing up and furling more difficult, as the sails have to be hauled up to the yards when full, rather than being blanketed by other sails in the usual way. It does not appear to be much of a problem, as there is always a large crew and the *Mir* has even rounded Cape Horn on a world cruise with no difficulty as far as I know.

I went aboard and was shown to my quarters where I met my new cabin mates. The cabins or "kubricks" as they are called in Russian are quite basic with twelve bunks on two levels with small lockers for clothes. Heads and showers are in a separate communal area. We introduced ourselves and found that six of us were British; five were German and one Belgian. All were middle aged or elderly; Julius the Belgian was in his seventies! A gentleman from Switzerland who was 95 arrived and tried to get a berth in the *Mir* but due to his age the captain refused. He got a berth eventually aboard the Dutch barque *Europa*. Being an accomplished artist he made many drawings during the race. We spent the first day getting to know our way around the ship and watching all the activity ashore. One of my cabin mates brought a newspaper aboard with the intriguing headline "Mir lost in space!" This referred to the Russian Space Station also called Mir which was in the news at the time. We had our first experience of Russian cuisine on arrival. Bean soup, lukewarm spaghetti (nicknamed rubber worms by our watch comedian Frank) with meatballs covered in grease! As Frank said, "it's just as well we're not here for the food". Some of us went shopping in Aberdeen, just in case this was what we could expect for the rest of the voyage. The mighty *Sedov* arrived and tied up alongside us. Frank had named her *"Sod Off"*. Until then we had thought the *Mir* was big but alongside *Sedov* she seemed almost delicate. *Sedov's* massive four mast barque rig and heavy "Cape Horn" gear contrasted with our lighter and more modern rig. The *Sedov* worked mostly in the South American nitrate and Australian grain trades and after the war was handed over to Britain who gave her to Russia as we had no use for her. This was just as well as otherwise she would almost certainly been scrapped. *Sedov* was the largest sailing ship afloat until the recent launch of the spectacular five mast full rigged passenger cruise ship the *Royal Clipper*.

The race started in the late afternoon and the *Malcolm Miller* led the fleet out of the harbour. This was a mark of respect as Aberdeen was her home port and the S.T.A. the host. The crowds along the shore were enormous and the press in helicopters and R.I.B.s were everywhere taking pictures. The wind was S.S.E. force 4 which was good for the square riggers; once the tugs cast us off and clear of the harbour we set all sail. Our captain Victor Antonov gave us all a short pep talk, promising that we were able to win and encouraging us all to do our best. We were in class A, and the start was amazing with *Sedov, Mir, Christian Radich, Statsraad Lehmkuhl, Sorlandet, Europa, Alexander von Humboldt, Pogoria, and Swan fan Makkum* all trying to get across the line first. We had an excellent start as our captain is a keen racing man and he really sails the *Mir* to win. With the wind force 4 on our starboard quarter we were soon making 10 knots. There was a great deal of trimming of braces and sheets until the watch officer was satisfied. They really sail this ship like a racing yacht! Over the first hour we steadily left the other ships astern and by dusk we were well ahead of *Sedov* and *Statsraad Lehmkuhl,* with the *Christian Radich* about two miles away on our starboard beam. The Dutch brigantine *Swan fan Makkum* was keeping up well but we steadily left them all astern. I was in the mizzen watch 08.00 to 12.00 and was appointed watch leader by Imke the ship's trainer whose job was to keep an eye on us, help us and explain anything we needed to know. She spoke good English and was very knowledgeable.

Our watch was under the bosun who was not very friendly and obviously regarded us as nuisances to be tolerated at best, or shouted at depending on his mood. Joan O'Neil the Tall Ship Friends U.K. organiser also sailed with us, but when tailing on a line she fell against a bollard and cracked her ribs. She was bandaged by our Russian doctor and confined to the hospital in a gimballed bunk for the rest of the race. She was very disappointed and in a lot of pain but managed to come on deck again after a few days.

The mighty Sedov

The next morning was fine again with a little more wind. Now S.E. force 5, we were running at 12 knots with everything set. That is all square sails – courses (except the cro'jack) lower and upper topsails, topgallants and royals, all jibs and staysails and spanker - 26 sails in total. On watch we were all kept busy under the watchful and strict eye of the bosun. One of our watch asked him what his problem was and why was he so bad tempered. The sobering reply was "because you have spent more for this voyage than I earn in six months and I haven't been paid since I left Russia!" As Imke had developed a heavy cold she asked me to take a class on the basics of square rig sailing in the training room for the English speakers in our watch. I was surprised how little knowledge some people had although they had sailed on square riggers before. Most of us ate what was provided at mealtimes although it was generally awful. I suppose we were hungry and the food was a great source of jokes and entertainment.

There was usually plenty left over and we could always rely on Otto, a large German nicknamed the "dustbin" to eat it up.

Two days out the wind fell light during the night. I came on watch at 20.00 to find the ship close hauled on the starboard tack making 4 to 5 knots. Our compass course was 335 degrees and up to then we had covered 260 miles in 24 hours, an average of 10.8 knots. There was a cadets' chart room for training, fully equipped with G.P.S., giro compass, log etc. that we had access to. We could therefore check the ship's position and speed whenever we wanted. Our midday position was 62.11N, 03.34E. The good news was that the *Sedov* was reported being 20 miles astern and no other ship was closer than 10 miles. I was on galley duty for two meals which involved serving both trainees and cadets and clearing up afterwards. The wind continued to head us and eventually we had to tack ship. I was impressed that we made this first tack in 8 minutes which is good for any square rigger. The wind fell lighter to force 2 to 3 from the north and I went aloft to the main lower topsail yard to watch the sun dipping below the horizon in a red and orange sky as we sailed through the North Sea oil fields. In fact the sun hardly set at all as we made our way north.

Friday 18th July. 06.30 all hands to tack ship. This was announced on the ships intercom - "sailing alarm, sailing alarm" in a strong Russian accent, enough to waken the dead. The wind was still light from the north and our speed was only 3 to 4 knots.

Mir close hauled

We tacked again this time in 7 minutes, the sun is up and the ship pointing well – 50 to 55 degrees apparent. Imke now recovered, gave us a Russian lesson for beginners which was quite amusing. She told us that Russian had more swear words than any other language; Frank wanted to learn a few to try out on the bosun! We spent most of the day tacking back and forth looking for wind and the Italian Naval yacht *Corsaro* could now be seen to starboard, with the Swedish sister schooners *Gladan* and *Falkan* on the horizon to port. These light conditions suited the smaller fore and aft vessels better. This was disappointing but of course we were really only interested in the class A ships. Our noonday position was 62.53N. 05.50E and although we had sailed 129 miles in the previous 24 hours we had made little headway. It freshened again in the late afternoon, still from the north as we made our way to windward at 9 to 10 knots. It did not last long however and soon we were becalmed again. To break the monotony our resident Russian folk group gave a concert. This was scheduled to happen earlier but we were told they were indisposed! Although the *Mir* is officially a "dry" ship we had hints that vodka may have been the reason. They were excellent and many of the Russian boys were visibly moved by the haunting sound and lyrics of traditional folk music which obviously meant much to them, as I am sure most of the cadets were homesick.

The next day, Saturday was disappointing. The sea was like glass and it was warm and sunny, The *Christian Radich* passed us far away to port where she had a light breeze and the *Statsraad Lehmkuhl* crossed ahead of us on starboard tack. Ships do come together in a calm; it was amazing that after 600 miles we were all so close. The race was now on again in earnest and we were all keyed up to beat the others. We tacked again three times during the night in light airs and hoped our superior windward performance would pay off. Gradually the wind increased again and during one tack the topgallant brace got jammed in the lead block, as the brace had not been properly flaked out on deck before tacking, which was not helped by dozens of cadets running over it. There was a lot of strong language from the bosun and others and we listened intently to see if we had learned anything at our Russian lesson! A sweepstake was held for the finishing time; we expected to finish early on Monday morning. I estimated that if the wind held we would finish around 04.15.

Monday 21st July – We crossed the finishing line at 06.30. Bruno the Swiss trainee won the sweepstake. When I came on watch at 08.00 the previous watch had already clewed up and furled all sails except the lower and upper topsails and fore and aft sails. We were all looking forward to Trondheim and even the bosun was smiling. We soon discovered that we were the first ship home in class A and our Captain's estimate of the final corrected times was *Christian Radich* 1st, *Statsraad Lehmkuhl* 2nd and *Mir* 3rd. This was later confirmed. We reckoned that if the wind had held all the way we would have easily won on corrected time. Nevertheless all hands were delighted with the result.

Our first place over the line was a pleasant birthday treat for Captain Antonov. We celebrated his birthday a few miles from Trondheim with a presentation of a large home made card and a string of paper ships, each with the name of a ship in the race. We all sang "Happy Birthday" together in different languages and the youngest girl aboard, a 17 year old from Glasgow give him a birthday kiss. He was quite overcome and embarrassed and thanked us all profusely. All sail was stowed, the ship cleaned from stem to stern and we motored up the fiord to the town. Lots of local boats came out to see us and our tug came alongside to take us into harbour. The tug was crewed by two blonde Norwegian girls, not the average tugboat crew one expects!

On watch aboard the Mir

Tied up in Trondheim the fleet was an impressive sight. The sun shone and the *Q.E.2* arrived providing a photogenic backdrop which was best appreciated from a high vantage point above the town with all the ships in the foreground. This was the 1,000 year celebrations of the city of

Trondheim and we had a great time meeting other crews and exploring the town. Most of the crews could not afford to eat ashore as a hamburger cost nearly £5 and a beer was £3.50. We were now so used to Russian food that most of us continued to eat aboard, as at least it cost nothing.

We had one excellent meal in Trondheim in the company of a French lady in her seventies whose father had been a pilot at Le Havre. She had always wanted to sail on a sailing ship and decided to do it while she was still able. She told us of a French speaking elderly gentleman who had joined the *Mir* in Aberdeen and asked her about the food. "How is the cheese selection and is there a good wine cellar aboard" he said. After she had picked herself up from the deck having collapsed with laughter, she gently explained that the cuisine was much more basic! Curiously the same gentleman who was elderly stayed aboard the *Mir* for almost a year.

The Tall Ships Race always finishes with the prize giving when all the crews parade through the streets; some in uniform and others in fancy dress. It was great to see so many young people of different nationalities, who a few years before could have been enemies marching together and making friends. This is what the Tall Ships Races are all about.

Prizegiving parade Trondheim

I heard that recently, one of the S.T.A. brigs had both Palestinian Muslims and Jewish Israelis aboard. That must be the ultimate proof of friendship and tolerance which sail training can produce. The procession was led by the *Statsraad Lehmkuhl* and first in line was an 88 year old Norwegian trainee who marched the whole way to the town square ringing a miniature ship's bell, while the *Churchill's* and *Miller's* boys and girls in fancy dress got involved with water fights en-route. It was noticeable that the British crews were the most extrovert. Our captain received our prize for 3rd place and a barbeque and party was held for the crews of all the ships. At midnight it was still light enough to read a newspaper and Frank and I sat outdoors in a dockside café drinking coffee and putting the world to rights.

I flew home content. To participate in the Tall Ships Race is an unforgettable experience at any time but particularly in a large square rigger. The thrill of feeling a large vessel moving at 12 knots or more and the sheer size of everything on board made all my other sailing seem tame in comparison. Once experienced, one always longs to go back to sea again. I am pleased to be able to say that this is now much easier than in the past.

The following year saw the Festival of the Sea at Portsmouth. I had joined the *Kruzenstern* in Dublin along with my nephew Colin at the finish of the Tall Ships Race. The *Kruzenstern* along with many others was going on to Portsmouth for one of the largest rallies of traditional sailing ships and yachts ever held in the U.K. The usual Tall Ship's festivities were going on when we arrived in Dublin. The crews were as good natured, noisy and enthusiastic as ever and this time the Mexican barque with the unpronounceable name of *Cuauhtemoc* was there. One could hardly miss them as along with the *Gloria* from Colombia and *Libertad* from Argentina there was Latin American music from live bands playing on their decks and their navy cadets were very popular, particularly with the Irish colleens. It was a long held ambition of mine to sail on a real "Cape Horner" and the *Kruzenstern* was the "real McCoy". I told a little of her history earlier this chapter. The *Kruzenstern* is in excellent condition, although over 70 years old. Apart from the accommodation she is hardly changed from her grain carrying days. The sheer size of masts yards and gear is the first thing I noticed on coming aboard. The deck is vast and there are "Jarvis" brace winches and capstans to ease sail handling. A Captain Jarvis of Dundee invented this winch in the latter days of sail which he designed to work the braces of sailing vessels. This was a great benefit as brace trimming could be achieved by a few men when otherwise a whole watch might be required. Brace winches and capstans were common in the last of the large windjammers when crews were ridiculously small and owners tried to squeeze the maximum effort from them at the lowest cost. The *Padua* as she was then called, along with the others of her type often went to sea with only 20 to 30 of a crew. Most were young including officers - in their teens or twenties. It was skilled seamanship learned the hard way that enabled them to make passages from Australia or South America round the Horn in some of the wildest waters in the world. They had no engines, radios or other modern navigational aids then; only charts, a magnetic compass, sextant and a primitive log but they had experience, they knew the sea and the winds and how to use them in ways which are now all but forgotten. Today of course the *Kruzenstern* has all the best navigational equipment, much is obligatory by the authorities now. She also has powerful engines as these ships have tight schedules to keep which would be impossible under sail only.

We settled in to our cabin which had 14 berths and came back on deck to watch as we were towed out of the harbour by two tugs. Once clear we were under our own power and joined the rest of the fleet to prepare for the start with the usual multitudes on the shore and hundreds of boats surrounding us. The wind was around force 4 which is not much for a ship like this. She really needs force 6 or more to really get going. All sail was set with amazing co-ordination from such a large crew. The watch officer giving commands with a whistle. There were over 200 people aboard, a far cry from the Cape Horn days! We trainees could only look on at first as the cadets worked the ship. Our chance to work on deck and go aloft would come later. Our companions were a mixed bunch, some Irish, some German and Randy an American airline pilot who had found the *Kruzenstern* on the Internet and decided he would like to sail in her.

The passage down the Irish Sea and round the Lizard was quiet and the winds were disappointingly light although from the north. I did however enjoy the experience and we all had little jobs to do to pass the time. The food aboard this ship was much better than in the *Mir,* apparently not all Russian ships are alike. (I have heard the food on the *Mir* has since improved!) We soon made new friends and looked forward to our arrival in Portsmouth. The sun shone and the cadets were kept hard at work scrubbing and holystoning the decks and washing paintwork, catching mackerel from the bowsprit and washing clothes when off watch. We drifted for most of the day then put a harbour stow on all sails and motored past the Isle of Wight. We made our way slowly up Spithead and docked at our pre-arranged berth at the Portsmouth Naval Dockyard. The crowds had already gathered. It was similar to the festival at Brest, as thousands of people walked round the historic dockyard to see the ships and other exhibits. It was fascinating to see the ships of our former enemies, Germany, Russia and Argentina tied up together in our formerly top secret historic naval base.

Aloft and furl - Kruzenstern

There was an amazing variety of happenings ashore with brass bands, air sea rescue displays, actors re-living the navy of Nelson's day and acting characters of Portsmouth 200 years before. The actual original topsail from *H.M.S. Victory* used at the Battle of Trafalgar was on display, as well as an incredible collection of model ships and all sorts of stalls selling everything from ice cream to marine trinkets; a real day out for all the family.

Kruzenstern – Washday at sea

Colin and I went over to the yacht basin where a large number of classic yachts were gathered. The O.G.A. had encouraged many boats to take part and we watched them arriving and sailing around the harbour from the high vantage point on our ship. The yacht harbour was packed with many famous yachts. I saw my brother Kenneth's old yacht *Tinkatoo* there and managed to have a look aboard. *Tinkatoo* is a Holman designed "Rummer" yawl and a fine cruising boat. Libby Purvis the journalist was her owner at that time and she told us that the boat had wintered at Kerrera the previous year and she knew my sister Joyce. Exhausted from all this activity, Colin and I eventually left the *Kruzenstern* at Portsmouth and took a train home to Glasgow.

By now I had the "Tall Ship Bug" and I was keen to experience one of the Norwegian ships which I had always admired. Through Tall Ship Friends again I booked a passage to Norway in the *Christian Radich* in 2003. She was at the Festival of the Sea at Leith which was smaller than the Portsmouth event, but interesting and well organised nevertheless. I joined the ship looking forward to better conditions and a friendlier crew than aboard the Russian vessels. I was not disappointed. The *Christian Radich* is one of the world's best known sailing ships. A three mast full rigged ship of 696 gross tons, 205 feet long, built in 1937 for sail training. She featured in the film "Windjammer" in the fifties and is a regular participant in the Tall Ships Races. As with other ships nowadays, anyone can apply to sail in her.

The *Christian Radich* is as well maintained as any yacht and the officers and crew have great pride in their ship. She has undergone a major refit and improvement programme and is as good as, or even better than when she was originally built. I got to know the bosun well who like most Scandinavians spoke almost perfect English. The accommodation is comfortable with berths and large lockers arranged dormitory style around the side of the ship in the half deck. The joiner work was obviously new in solid pine, no plywood to be seen. Our first meal was a very pleasant change from the Russian ships, a typical Smorgasbord with a huge variety of cold meats, fish and salads. On introducing myself to other trainees, a gentleman from Blairgowrie - Giles Atkins recognised my surname and asked me if I had sailed on the *Malcolm Miller* I did not know him but he had mistaken me for my brother Kenneth as they had both been watch officers on the *Miller* many years before. Giles and I had much in common and he introduced me to Norwegian friends in Oslo as his wife is from there. We locked out of Leith docks about midnight after watching the finale of the festival with fireworks and music and motored into the North Sea as the wind was very light from the south.

Early the next morning I was on lookout duty on the forecastle. The sun was starting to warm the air and the sea was calm. I looked down at the bow wave and saw six or seven dolphins swimming just ahead of us. They were able to keep at exactly the same speed as the ship and sometimes dived and surfaced again in the same positions, one or two would shoot off away from the bow and suddenly return to swim so close to the bow that it appeared they would be hurt as we were travelling through the water at about 9 knots but they were quite safe. Suddenly they disappeared as quickly as they had come. On watch we stood lookout, made safety checks every hour and took the wheel. The wind was still elusive but at least it was sunny and warm. This is not the North Sea as we know it, we all said. Eventually the wind came away from the South and we got sailing at last. We had a very pleasant passage across the North Sea and tied up at Risor a small, attractive Norwegian fishing port. A walk ashore was called for to stretch our legs and we climbed the hill overlooking the town where old German gun positions from the war were still to be seen. There was a beautiful view over the harbour and outlying islands and the *Christian Radich* looked tiny in the distance. On coming down again I noticed a small boatyard and curious as ever, walked in to find they were building Colin Archer type yachts in traditional oak. Colin Archer was a Scotsman who immigrated to Norway in the 19th Century and developed a seaworthy type of sailing boat for the Norwegian lifeboat service. Some of the original Colin Archer boats survive to this day such as the original boat named *Colin Archer* of 1893 but there have been many new ones built as yachts and it was good to see the old skills still being used. On arriving back at the harbour I saw a yacht with an Irish ensign and on saying hello I met the husband and wife crew who were on a cruise from Cork to Norway, Denmark, Germany and Holland before sailing home to Ireland. The owner's name was Brian Cudmore, cousin of Harold Cudmore the well known Irish yachtsman. We chatted for a while and they knew many of my old Irish friends. Back aboard our ship we set sail for Oslo and arrived under sail in Oslo Fjord in perfect weather the next evening. We tied up at the ship's usual berth in the city centre as this is her home port. I met Giles' relatives and was entertained to dinner at their home. Oslo is a beautiful city and as it was a weekend there were literally hundreds of boats on the water. They say that everyone in Norway has a second house on an island and a boat! It is certainly a prosperous place and Norway is not a member of the E.C.! The *Christian Radich* is a delightful ship and I flew home after seeing the sights and saying goodbye to my hosts and look forward to returning to friendly Norway again someday.

The *Eye of the Wind* is probably my favourite square rigged vessel. I had often seen her at Tall Ships Races and heard of her voyages around the world (4 times). In 2000 I heard that she was in Penzance and that her owner and skipper "Tiger" Timbs was considering putting her on the market. I had always been keen to sail her and I applied for a berth as I did not want to miss an opportunity which may not come again. I discovered that the *Eye* is special. Many people have sailed aboard her on multiple cruises and she is known as a "happy ship". I travelled by train to Penzance from Glasgow which is an incredibly long journey, to find my way to the dock laden down with my sea bag. There she was, it was September and getting dark but she looked beautiful and purposeful in the glow of the pier lights. I stepped aboard and entered the deck saloon where Tiger and some of the crew were sitting around the table. The *Eye* is relatively small compared to the other square riggers I had sailed in, at 106 feet on deck and 150 gross tons. She was built in Brake on the river Weser in Germany in 1911 as a topsail schooner for the South American hide trade and named *Friedrich*. An engine was installed in 1923 and the topmasts and yards were sent down a few years later. She traded in the Baltic and North Sea for many years under Swedish ownership re-named *Merry* but in 1969 a fire broke out in the engine room and it seemed that her life was over. In 1973 Tiger found her, patched her up and took her to Faversham in Essex where over a three year period he restored the ship and rigged her as a true brigantine. This rig has square sails on both masts but the rig commonly known as brigantine or hermaphrodite brig has square sails only on the foremast. She was re-named the *Eye of the Wind* and Tiger personally skippered her for 27 years. The first voyage was a circumnavigation of the Globe averaging 100 miles a day on the 18,000 mile passage to Sidney. She then became the flagship for "Operation Drake" which was a two year round the world scientific expedition involving some 400 young people from 27 nations under the patronage of H.R.H. Prince Charles, finishing in London in1980. The *Eye* has appeared in several feature films including "Blue Lagoon, "Savage Islands", "Taipan", "Desperate Fortune" and "White Squall". In 1990 she sailed across the Southern Ocean to participate in the celebration of Pitcairn Island's 200 years settlement and in 1991 she made her most adventurous voyage, from Sydney homeward round Cape Horn to Lisbon to take part in the company of the largest Tall Ships fleet of the century - the Columbus Grand Regatta to the Americas, finally arriving home after 11 months. A well travelled old lady indeed!

The Eye of the Wind

The *Eye* has always had the reputation of being a friendly ship and from the moment I stepped aboard I felt at home. To my surprise, I bumped into Frank my old shipmate from the *Mir* as soon as I opened the deckhouse door. He had sailed in the ship before and was looking forward to the proposed passage across the channel to France. The crew totalled 27 and as in most of these vessels, quite international and young, mainly British, Australian and Canadian, so no language problems. The oldest person was Lesley from Edinburgh, Frank's friend who had celebrated her 80th birthday aboard the *Eye* the previous year. At her age she did not do anything on deck but enjoyed watching the goings on and helped out in the galley. The cook was Jill who produced really excellent meals whatever the weather. I was told that she had run her own restaurant but sold up to come on the ship. Due to the size of the ship, trainees could be much more "hands on", getting involved with sail handling much more than in the some of the larger ships, where sometimes there are too many people aboard.

We got underway after the captain's briefing at 16.00 hours on Sunday 17th September. I chose the middle watch, from 08.00 to 12.00. We set all sail and steered a course of 190 degrees for the Lizard. The wind was westerly force 3 to 4 but it eased off as night fell. On watch I steered and stood lookout, there was a long Atlantic swell and more wind was forecast. By morning the wind had veered to the northwest and increased to force 6.

We had reduced sail during the night but the ship was now logging 8 knots and some of the trainees had succumbed to seasickness. My cabin mate from Wales had been sick during the night in the bunk below me which was most unpleasant when coming off watch. The morning continued with an uncomfortable beam sea causing the ship to roll badly but we made good progress until mid morning when the wind died away and veered until it was dead aft. More of our watch were sick and only three trainees appeared on deck when called. – Frank, Sarah and myself. At 11.00 we went aloft to set the main topsail which was quite hard as she was rolling heavily and the footropes were slippery. At times like these you can only imagine how it must have been on the old Cape Horners in the Southern Ocean with tiny, undernourished crews, endless gales and ice in the rigging! One of the trainees Albert was sitting on the skylight watching the sea when suddenly he tumbled face first into the lee scuppers. Fortunately Peter the engineer was nearby and pulled him up. He appeared to have fainted but recovered quite quickly. Nothing seemed to be wrong except for a cut on his forehead. We put it down to fatigue and seasickness. We were heading for St. Malo and the wind gradually eased to force 3 and the sea abated, visibility deteriorated and it stared to rain. We had hoped to dock at St. Malo before midnight but were too late to lock in, so we anchored outside at 23.30. All hands went to bed except the anchor watch and had a good nights sleep.

On locking into the harbour basin we saw the new Jubilee Trust barque *Tenacious* in the harbour. Built in timber by volunteers she is the largest wooden ship built in the U.K. for many years. At 214 feet in length, she is specially designed, like the *Lord Nelson* to accommodate disabled people who would otherwise never be able to sail on such a ship. The day was spent shopping and looking around the town which is picturesque with ancient city walls and fascinating narrow streets. I came across a tiny shop where model sailing boats were being made on the premises and sold by a rather grumpy individual. The models were good but he gave the impression of not really wanting to sell any. In the evening all hands except Tiger met for a meal where Jill and some of the other extroverts took over the restaurant much to the bemusement of the locals.

Back aboard and underway at 10.00 the next morning bound for St Peter's Port in Guernsey. It was a beautiful day with a south westerly force 4. Under all sail and everyone in good spirits with seasickness and hangovers forgotten, Jill produced "Moules Marinere" for lunch with fresh St. Malo mussels. We left Jersey to starboard as the wind fell light again but this time the sky looked more threatening and the forecast was S to S.E., 5 to 6. Tiger decided to anchor off St. Peter's Port in Guernsey and during the night the wind came away strong from the South East. In the morning it was fairly howling in the rigging and our wind speed indicator registered over 30 knots and even 42 knots for a short time. The Brixham Trawler *Provident* came out of St Peter's Port under mizzen and staysail heading home across the Channel. There was no question of going ashore, and Jim the mate gave knot tying lessons to pass the time. We weighed anchor eventually and motored out directly into the wind and steep seas until laying our course for Brixham. The main staysail, inner jib and fore topsail were set before I came off watch. The weather brightened and wind eased to allow us to set more sail, all except the nock staysail. The seas gradually died down and we had good sailing weather across the Channel. In the dark at 01.00 on Friday morning we anchored in Brixham bay and after a quiet night woke up to a beautiful autumn day with sunshine and light winds. Brixham is an interesting town and birthplace of the famous Brixham sailing trawlers. A group of enthusiasts have managed to gather a number of these historic vessels together at a special pontoon berth in the harbour. I understand this was made possible by grant funding. It was a fine sight to see the *Vigilence, Provident, Leader, Pilgrim* and *Golden Vanity* back in their home port and able to race again. I met Bill Wakefield of the association who was working on *Pilgrim* and told me about the scheme and their plans for the future. We explored the town and on returning to the ship, found the crew had scrubbed the decks, cleaned the paintwork and polished the brass. We got underway after clearing a fouled anchor and sailed west past Dartmouth where we saw the *Soren Larsen* heading up channel inshore from us. The *Soren Larsen* had featured in the TV series "The Onedin Line" and Tiger was friendly with the captain and crew as the ships had sailed together on Operation Drake. By the next morning we were sailing quietly with all sail set round the Longships light to head into St. Ives where we anchored at 12.30. Ashore again, to look around this little port and back on board for an excellent roast lamb dinner. From St. Ives we sailed back round Land's End to Penzance. Good sailing weather again with all sails set until we stowed everything to motor into the harbour lock at 13.00 on Sunday. Some of us went to the Methodist church in the evening and we had a great farewell meal aboard late; so ended our short autumn cruise.

 Some new crew members came aboard to prepare the ship for a transatlantic voyage. We left the *Eye* saddened by the fact that Tiger had decided to sell her and retire to Australia. It was understandable that he should want to retire after so many years aboard, but we were all apprehensive about the ship's future. Would she be sold to someone who would change her? There were rumours that she would become a private yacht but no-one really knew. If Tiger knew he was keeping it to himself.

It turned out that we had no need to be concerned. The *Eye of the Wind* was sold to a Danish/American businessman who took her to Denmark for substantial alterations and improvements. She was indeed to be his private vessel but there would still be opportunities to sail in her. Her final voyage with Tiger was from Bermuda to Demark and in 2001 the work commenced. It is to Ole the owner and his captain Svend's credit, that the work was carried out most sympathetically and in no way detrimental to the historic character of the ship. The *Eye* was rejuvenated with some new bottom plates, new timber deck, new engine and generator, new navigational equipment, new accommodation with more spacious double cabins and en-suite facilities, air conditioning and heating and completely new rigging and sails. Although the *Eye* was not in bad condition these improvements have added many years to her life. She is more seaworthy and comfortable as a result and complies with all the current regulations. The ship can now accommodate up to twelve trainees/passengers and an annual sailing programme is in force with Diane Parsons still managing the U.K. shore office.

In 2004 I decided to see for myself what the *Eye* was like under the new ownership. I knew she was in British waters so I decided to join her for a short voyage. I flew to Dublin to meet the ship at Dunlaoghaire where she was lying alongside the south pier near the National Yacht Club. I met Svend the captain and his wife Gitte who were very friendly and hospitable. They are Danish and had previously run their own Baltic Trader as a charter vessel in Copenhagen. I was introduced to Ole the owner who spends most of the summer aboard when he is not at his home in California and has his own private quarters aboard. He is a most interesting gentleman and I enjoyed many conversations with him. As before the crew were international from Denmark, Holland, Canada, Australia, and England. Surprisingly there were more girls than boys among the permanent crew and very efficient and knowledgeable they were too. On the voyage the trainees or voyage crew as they are called, in other words the paying guests, were mainly from England with one Australian lady, the mate's mother. On meeting everyone I had no more worries about the change of ownership. Some sceptics had said that the *Eye* would never be the same as before but I found a really friendly atmosphere aboard and young and old worked well together. As usual there was a ship's comedian - Melvyn, a yachtsman who had retired from business. He is also a motorbike enthusiast and he proudly showed us photos of himself on his Harley Davidson at rallies. Melvyn has a very dry sense of humour which caused some hilarious moments when some of his jokes were a mystery to those crew members unacquainted with British humour but very funny to the rest of us. He would come out with remarks at the most unexpected moments. The other trainee was Fred who was a very active seventy plus and had sailed in the *Eye* before.

In Dunlaoghaire we watched yachts taking part in the evening racing and I was surprised how many class racing boats were there. A large number of Dragons and other dayboat classes were out and I was particularly interested in the old Dublin Bay 24's. These beautiful Milne designed sloops were destined to go to France. A charter company in the South of France had bought the whole fleet of I think, seven boats and they were due to be shipped out a few weeks later. I heard that they held their farewell regatta a few weeks before. I asked about the fate of the Dublin Bay 21's. These are local Milne one designs, rigged as gaff cutters which raced as a class for many years. Most of the boats needed serious work done and they were all brought together for restoration. It seems however that this plan has fallen through and I heard that all the boats are stored in a field near Arklow. If nothing is done soon they will be lost forever.

The port authorities told us that we had to be out of the harbour by 08.00 the following morning as a naval vessel was due in and they needed the berth. This was surprising as the quay was huge and there would have been plenty of room for two destroyers. We moved out anyway and anchored in Scotsman's Bay near the harbour. We spent the morning ashore and I visited the Royal Irish Yacht Club which I had not been in for many years. The clubhouse was as magnificent as ever with wonderful paintings, brass cannons on the terrace and spotless tables with shining silverware laid out in the dining room for lunch. This is a yacht club as it should be; it was like something out of a period film. The main change though was that the harbour has been almost completely filled up by a new marina where previously the club moorings lay. This has caused the old custom of inviting visiting yachts to use the club's facilities to cease. In the past every visiting yacht which anchored or picked up a club mooring received a formal invitation card inscribed with the yacht's name delivered by the club boatman a short time after arrival. This offered the visiting skipper and crew temporary membership and the use of all the club facilities during their stay in Dunlaoghaire. The club maintains a visitor's book and I asked to see some of the old books from the sixties and seventies. I found my late father in law's Colin Lang's signature who sailed to Dunlaoghaire in *Nomad II* and visited the club with his family including my wife Vivien on 26th July 1969. I also saw *Cruinnaig III, Mingary, Stornoway, Sea Bear, Seewolf* and other Clyde yachts of that time who had been there. I could not see the entry for our visit in *Wye* in 1968 as the book for that period was stored in the club archives. I looked round the yachts in the marina but came away a little depressed as all I could see was the usual collection of plastic cruisers just like in any other marina today.

Once back aboard we noticed that the Irish navy had not arrived and the harbour berth was still empty. Eventually a small patrol boat came in, why they wanted us out when there was plenty of room was a mystery. I was allocated to the green watch and had a cabin to myself. We got underway at 05.25 on Saturday morning, setting all sail on course for Douglas on the Isle of Man. As we had plenty of time we sailed slowly in light southerly winds up the Irish Sea. The general plan was to call in at Campbeltown before going up the Clyde to Glasgow, as Ole had friends he wanted to meet there. It was good to see the new sails which were in the same tan colour as before. This was always a feature of the *Eye* and are kinder on the eyes in the tropics. We enjoyed the sail handling and various jobs aboard. Our cook Kirsten was Danish and produced excellent meals often refusing help in the galley as she preferred to do everything herself. The galley had been re-equipped with a new cooker, fridge, freezer etc. and is much easier to work in than before. I was surprised how little shipping we saw and how few fishing boats, perhaps a sign of the times! Svend showed me all the new navigational gadgets including the large screen G.P.S. and electronic charts, linked to the "state of the art" radar. Ole also told me of some of the problems incurred during the refit that cost more than the purchase price of the ship.

The forecast was for strong south or south easterly winds but the sky looked settled and the glass was high. The wind gradually increased to force 4 during the day and the captain decided to set our stunsails. These sails properly called studding sails are not often seen today. They became popular in the tea clipper days and are square sails which extend the rig beyond the yard arms to provide extra sail area downwind. A stunsail is set with a spar at the head sliding out from the topsail or topgallant yard. The foot is sheeted to a lower spar attached to the yard. This sail can be very effective but is not easy to set or hand. I only know of three ships which carry stunsails today these are the *Europa,* the *Stad Amsterdam* and of course the *Eye of the Wind.* Two of the girls, Mie the bosun, and Sarah knew what to do and sat on the yard sorting out the gear, eventually getting the sail to set properly. All went well and we picked up speed as the wind was now dead aft force 5 in brilliant sunshine, perfect sailing conditions!

We handed the stunsails without difficulty and went aloft to furl all the other sails before motoring into Douglas where we berthed alongside the long pier. Mel, Fred and I went ashore to explore the town but were disappointed. The dock area was uninspiring and the cafes and pubs were full of noisy teenagers and loud music, so we returned to the ship for a pleasant evening with the older crew members as the youngsters wanted to make the most of Saturday night ashore.

Sunday dawned warm and sunny again with a nice Southerly force 4 breeze. We got underway leisurely at 11.00 and motored against the wind round the south of the island until we could steer a northerly course. All square and fore and aft sails were set by 14.00 and we had a wonderful day sailing up the Irish Sea. We attempted to set the stunsails again but this time they were temperamental as the halyard and sheet fouled and we gave up.

It was also gradually clouding over and the forecast was poor. It did not come to anything though and by evening we had S.E. force 3 which died away off the Rhinns of Galloway. The wind veered to S.S.W. during the night and visibility was very clear. On watch we spent the time identifying stars and watching passing ships' lights. After breakfast the next morning Ole and Svend asked me about the possibility of going up the Clyde to Glasgow. My response was that Glasgow is not the best place for a small sailing vessel and it would take a long time to get up the river. Why not try another port on the mainland?

We decided that Largs would be the best place and I called Carolyn at Largs Yacht Haven to ask if we could berth there. We were in some doubt as we thought the *Eye* might be too long and draw too much but Carolyn said it should be OK. We sailed steadily up the Clyde with Ailsa Craig abeam and sailed into Largs Channel where several yachts came over for a better look. You don't see square riggers on the Clyde every day! Once off the marina we called Carolyn again and she confirmed they were waiting for us and we started to motor gently towards the marina entrance. From our vantage point on the poop it seemed almost impossible. As we came through the entrance Ole turned to me and said "Are you quite sure this is OK Gordon?" My diplomatic reply was "I can only go by what the marina manager says; if Carolyn says it's OK it's OK!" We crept past the visitors berth and at the far side we could then see that there was more space than we originally thought. Svend was at the wheel and with an excellent show of seamanship turned the ship in her own length using the bow thrusters and gently laid the *Eye* alongside a pontoon. Our bowsprit overhung the next lane but we were safely berthed, heading seaward for an easy departure. A stream of yachting people came along to see us and many were shown over the ship. Carolyn put some of our brochures on display at the marina office to let yachtsmen know that they too can sail on a square rigger. So my mini voyage came to an end at my home port. I thoroughly enjoyed my time in the *Eye* again and promised to make another voyage perhaps in Scottish waters another year. Gitte told me they intend to come back to Scotland in 2005.

Stunsail set and drawing

Chapter 9 - Loose Ends

Many yachtsmen have very little knowledge of square rig and how the gear works. At first sight the sheer number of lines around the mast and running down to the bulwarks seem impossible. What are they all for? How do you know which is which? Can a square rigger sail to windward? Is square rig not very inefficient? These are some of the questions we often get asked. I will try to answer these and explain a little about the rig.

It must first be remembered that square rig is intended primarily for trade wind sailing. The sailing ships of the past used the trade winds and set their courses to take the maximum advantage of them. This means that sailing vessels often had to sail indirect courses to their destination when steamers could sail on a straight rumb line course. For example a sailing ship crossing the Atlantic had to sail south to the Azores to try and pick up the north east trade winds before steering west. A power vessel can simply steer due west from the Lizard. For sailing before the wind in a large vessel there is no better rig than square sails. They are easier to handle as the rig is split up into more easily handled sails than a few large ones such as in a large schooner. There is no possibility of danger from gybing as in for and aft rig and although it is necessary to go aloft to loose gaskets or furl, the sails can be clewed up from the deck. The development of square rig progressed slowly but steadily over the 19th century and into the 20th. The tea clippers are considered to be the final development of square rig which could hardly be improved. These clippers were designed for speed as their existence depended on bringing their cargos to the market as quickly as possible. The ships however were relatively small unlike their successors and carried adequate crews. The *Cutty Sark* at Greenwich is the sole surviving tea clipper in existence. The large sailing vessels of the early 20th century had to work with very small crews. Image a ship like the *Sedov* or *Kruzenstern* sailing thousands of miles for months with a crew no larger than that of the *Eye of the Wind*!

These large steel built vessels were built to carry as much cargo as possible and although not built for speed could nevertheless make fast passages. Their rigs were cleverly designed to be handled by small crews and mechanical devices such as brace and halyard winches certainly helped. In those days a deep sea sailing vessel was completely self sufficient. As long as they had enough food and water they could stay at sea for many months and the long voyages from Australia or the west coast of South America to Europe made self sufficiency a necessity. The carpenter, bosun and sailmaker could usually undertake all necessary repairs and there are even accounts of ships managing major repairs in a remote part of the world after a dismasting. The *Glenlee* is a fine example of a latter day sailing vessel. She has been restored with assistance from the National Lottery Fund and is berthed in Glasgow. The *Glenlee* is a steel three mast barque and is what was known as a "bald headed" vessel. This means that she sets no royal sails. On the fore and main mast from the deck up the sails are course, lower topsail, upper topsail, lower topgallant and upper topgallant. As she is a barque a spanker is set on the mizzen mast which is a fore and aft gaff sail with a topsail. The reason for the development of this rig from the once ubiquitous ship rig was easier handling as when the *Glenlee* was built sailing ships were already in serious decline and they were only suited to bulk cargos which did not have to be delivered quickly. In an attempt make a profit and to stave off the inevitable, ships were designed to be operated with as few people as possible.

The Glenlee in Greenock at the Tall Ships Race

The *Glenlee* has been restored as close as possible to her original condition and one can see how the ship was built, how the cargo was stowed and how the crew lived aboard. A visit to the ship is well worth making to understand something of life at sea under sail in those days.

Likewise the *Cutty Sark* mentioned earlier is the only complete example of a 19th century clipper ship in the world.

To get back to the rig; although the gear looks very complicated there are general rules concerning the layout of the numerous lines. Halyards are used to hoist certain square yards and fore and aft sails such as jibs and staysails just as in a yacht. Braces control the horizontal movement of the yards. Every sail has sheets which control the clews; square sails are sheeted to the yard immediately below or to the deck in the case of courses (the lowest square sails). Fore and aft sails are sheeted to the deck just as in a yacht. Buntlines and clewlines run from the foot of the square sails through blocks on the yards to run down to the side of the ship where there are used to "clew up" the sails prior to furling. This means that the wind can be spilled from a sail by lowering the yard and clewing it up, thus reducing sail quickly. Likewise setting sail is this process in reverse. Some new ships have standing topsail, topgallant and royal yards without halyards which I described in a previous chapter. The *Mir* and her sisters are rigged this way. This reduces clutter on deck but is in my opinion not as easy for a small crew. Other rigging includes lifts to the end of the yards, downhauls to pull the hoisting yards down when lowering, also found on fore and aft sails. The whole rig is supported by various forestays running from different points on the masts forward to the bowsprit or next mast, shrouds supporting the masts at each side and substantial backstays supporting the rig from aft. Ratlines are ropes or wood battens fixed to the shrouds to enable the crew to climb aloft and footropes are wires suspended from the yards for the crew to stand on while handling the sails.

These are the basics and the number and sizes of different pieces of rigging can vary from ship to ship. For example a small vessel like the *Eye of the Wind* will have fewer buntlines for each sail than a large barque like the *Sedov*. The basic layout of the gear is very similar in every ship. For example lines belayed on the pin rails by the bulwarks along the side of the ship are always in the same order starting from forward with the lowest sails and finishing aft with the highest; so the fore course buntlines will be found at the forward end of the pin rail and the royal buntlines at the after end. The same rule applies to halyards and other running gear and similar rules apply to the lines belayed on the fife rails round the masts. All this has evolved over centuries and seamen both in the past and today can move from ship to ship and nationality to nationality, even without any knowledge of the language spoken aboard.

It is assumed by many yachtsmen that square riggers cannot sail to windward. It is true that the rig is intended for downwind sailing but many ships would never have survived without some windward ability, as many ships had to beat to windward off a lee shore in the days before engines. Typically a square rigged vessel can point to around 60 degrees. The reasons for this are the inability to square the yards far enough fore and aft to enable the ship to point closer to the wind and also the great windage of the masts, yards and rigging. Some modern vessels such as the *Mir* can brace the yards up sharper than older rigs and can sail to around 50 degrees to the wind which makes a big difference and is one of the reasons why the *Mir* wins so many races. In the past many coastal sailing vessels combined square rig with fore and aft rig which produced rigs such as brigantines, topsail schooners and barquentines. (See the appendix for illustrations of different rigs.) These were generally easier to handle and sailed better to windward than full rigged vessels such as brigs or ships.

    Tacking a square rigger is more complicated than a fore and aft vessel. The procedure is for the helmsman to wait for the watch officer's command. He must anticipate the best moment to tack, taking into account the wind strength and sea conditions. It must be remembered that tacking in heavy weather can be dangerous and the rig is designed for downwind sailing and there are massive backstays supporting the masts from aft but only the forestays from forward. When the command is given the helmsman turns the ship's head into the wind. At the same time the spanker is hauled to weather and the main yards swung round for the new tack. The fore mast yards and headsails are left in their position, coming aback and helping to push the ship's head round. Once the ship is on the other tack the fore mast yards and fore and aft sails are trimmed for the new tack. In heavy weather there is a danger that the ship could get caught in irons and that the wind pressure on the wrong side of the square sails could cause damage. For this reason square riggers often "wear ship" rather than tack which is known to yachtsmen as "gybing". Tacking a large square rigged vessel can sometimes take half an hour or more but the *Mir* can tack in five minutes in good weather with a well trained crew.

    I have been blessed in my sailing in that I have never experienced seriously bad weather. No seaman enjoys gales and storms. Some people assume that there is a great thrill in them but bad weather means more hard work for those on watch, being called on deck during the watch below or having to repair sails and broken gear. In the past the extreme discomfort of cold and being unable to get dry, with all one's clothes soaked for days on end must have been grim. Just ask any fisherman what he thinks of bad winter weather! In the same way many people assume sailors love the sea. This is also a misconception. We love being at sea, it is for both professional and amateur a unique way of life, but really we love the ships, the skill of handling them and the life at sea. There is great pride and satisfaction in being part of the crew of a beautiful and successful sailing ship which I am sure is not the case with many modern powered vessels. The amateur yachtsman gains great satisfaction in navigating his little vessel to a new port and really experiences a sense of adventure in doing so. Many sailors get a lot of satisfaction from making improvements and maintaining their boats, I certainly do. There are many facets to sailing and for traditional sailors like me the opportunities today are greater than ever before.

I have mainly concentrated on the yachts and ships so far in this book but without people there would be no ships. I have met many interesting men and women (mainly men) who could be called "characters" These are usually colourful, larger than life individuals who have become well known in their lifetimes. They can be found in big ships and small yachts, in the merchant service or fishing boats. There is something about life at sea which produces such interesting people. Some of this humour was captured by Neil Munro in his "Para Handy Tales" which are typical of the seafaring people of the West of Scotland at that time. I recall some of the yachting characters from my youth. In the fifties there seemed to be many more eccentric and loveable old (to us) sailing types than nowadays. I think their personalities mirrored their boats. As the yachts of those days were individual and different so also were their owners. The boats of today seem bland in comparison, what about the owners? I knew Ian Young of *Arcturus,* Tam Reid of *Gunna* and David Reekie of *Dirk II* well. All had similar sized two masted yachts. There was always great rivalry between them and they even organised a private race around Ailsa Craig. Tam Reid won it and the prize cheque was framed and fixed to *Gunna's* bulkhead beside the whisky and gin bottles where they were sure to be seen. Ian Young was a kindly man with a very loud voice. Tam Reid who owned the Paisley based Reid Gear Company and had spent some years as a ship's engineer in his youth had an extremely colourful vocabulary. David Reekie also known as the Scottish Soldier due to his wartime experiences was also an engineer from Paisley and related to Ian. My father was friendly with all three and *Northward* was a racing rival. When Ian, Tam, David and Bill with Harold all got together aboard one of the boats of an evening, you could hardly hear yourself think. It was impossible to get a word in edgeways as they all shouted to outdo Ian and usually did not listen to what the others were saying.

Most of our C.C.C. friends took part in all the events including the Tobermory Race which was a highlight of the season. Most were family boats and wives and children sailed for their summer holidays. This has completely changed today. As soon as they are old enough children go their own way and the friendly type of racing we used to enjoy has become much more serious and keen "go faster" sailors who sleep ashore at night rather than on their boats have taken over the racing scene. There were many other characters. As a child I remember seeing the eccentric Glasgow property millionaire A.E Pickard coming aboard the Clyde Steamer *Talisman* wearing a mini kilt over his trousers with a large tartan tammy on his head and trailing a toy dog on wheels behind him! He was certainly a colourful character. My late father in law Colin Lang in his ketch *Nomad II* with his friends Eric Whittaker from Yorkshire and Ninian Sanderson were also characters in their own ways. Ninian had been a successful racing driver for Ecurie Ecosse winning the Le Mans 24 hour race in Jaguars. He took up sailing and raced his 8 metre cruiser racer *Debbie* successfully. He was much misunderstood as he could be very aggressive but also a kind friend. It was always interesting to visit his motor dealership in Great Western Road in Glasgow where he was usually in conversation with well known personalities from the Scottish sporting or entertainment world. Colin and Eric along with a few others latterly moored their boats at Crinan where there was always a party on one or other of the yachts at weekends. Some of the funniest and most interesting characters were the professional yacht skippers. John McArthur from Rothesay, the Currie Brothers from Tignabruaich, the Shearers, Jimmy (Jimmack) Jeffrey and many others could tell stories which kept you laughing all night. I will not attempt to relate them here as they were really only funny in the telling but I will try and remember one of John McArthur's.

One day at the fishing, the crew of a Tarbert boat went ashore in Caradale for a dram after the week's work. Young Dougal was usually completely useless the next day after he had enjoyed a night out and the skipper, his uncle warned him of the dangers. Dougal had a relation who was a minister and on a rare occasion when he went to church, he heard a sermon warning of the evils of drink and that the devil himself would come after those who imbibed. Memories of "Tam o Shanter" would come to mind from time to time but he usually dismissed them with another drink. His skipper was getting somewhat fed up with Dougal and one night he hatched a plan. Dougal arrived back aboard in his usual condition and fell down the hatch to the fo'csle. Stumbling around in the dark he tried to undress, bumping into things. He clumsily struck a match and to his horror saw a face with a white beard and horror of horrors two horns! Convinced that "auld nick" was waiting for him, he scrambled up the ladder and tumbled ashore, not to be seen again until the morning. The skipper and the others had been hiding and could hardly contain themselves. When Dougal appeared later the next day, he had learned his lesson. The billy goat had by then been returned to its owner and Dougal never touched another drop. Talking of goats there used to be a flock of wild goats on the Holy Isle. John McArthur once when fishing off the east side saw the lighthouse keeper being chased by a few goats along the shore! I don't know If the goats are still her since the island became a Buddhist retreat but I wonder what an animal loving Buddhist would do if he was chased?

Although the Clyde characters were mostly men there were a few notable women. I described Irene McLaughlan from Luing in a previous chapter but must mention Elizabeth Todrick. Elizabeth worked in McGruer's as a boatbuilder all her life and was an experienced craftswoman. She owned *Ayrshire Lass* a Fife gaff cutter which she sailed engineless for many years. Elizabeth is still alive at the time of writing but is now very elderly. When younger she was as tough as, or tougher than any of the men she worked or sailed with and stood no nonsense from them. I remember once seeing *Ayrshire Lass* aground on a rock with Elizabeth up to her chest in the water with the bowsprit over her shoulder trying to push her off while her two male companions sat in the cockpit! Another strong lady was Miss Edwards owner of *Sibyl of Cumae* another Fife yacht who always took part in the C.C.C. races in my youth.

The Tarbert Loch Fyne fisherman had their own way of speaking which often puzzled outsiders. They used the expression "aye" in almost every conversation and "aye" could mean anything from agreement, cynicism, a question, an acknowledgement or even a greeting. It was said that Tarbert men could communicate with just that one word. Tarbert was of course a great fishing port at one time. In the days of the herring skiffs it was said that you could walk across the harbour on the decks of the boats. These days are long gone and the fishing fleet is a shadow of its former self. The whole of the Kintyre peninsula was involved in the fishing. Ardrishaig, Loch Gilphead, Tarbert, Caradale and Campbelltown were all important when the Loch Fyne herring were plentiful. The West of Scotland like other places had its own local boat types and the "Loch Fyne Skiff" was the model for the herring and line fishing boats in the past. These were typically around 30 feet long with the characteristic "Loch Fyne" stern - a steeply raked sternpost with outboard rudder and the hull planking bent tightly to form the round stern. The boats were usually built in larch with varnished topsides and in the heyday of the Loch Fyne herring there were hundreds working in the Firth of Clyde. They were rigged with a standing lugsail and small jib on a bowsprit with a small forecastle for the crew. They were handy boats and had good windward capability which is necessary in the Scottish lochs. There were also the smaller line skiffs. These were usually around 18 feet, open boats of similar design but with a dipping lugsail. John McArthur's father worked one of these boats from his home at St. Ninian's bay in Bute. Two men would go out line fishing until the boat was fully loaded. This could take several days in summer or winter and they were completely dependent on the wind or muscle power if it was calm. They were much tougher in those days! Further north there were other variations of the pointed stern fishing boats, from the Sgoths of Outer Isles, to the common skiffs from all over the west. On the east coast the famous Zulus, Skaffies and Fifies are similar and all these types have much in common with Scandinavian boats, probably due to the occupation by the Vikings in the 13th century. Unfortunately there are very few surviving original boats. Some have been converted to yachts and a few yachts built on skiff lines have been built. Unlike other parts of the U.K. where unwanted boats are abandoned in mud berths or sheltered rivers where someone could eventually restore them, Scottish fishermen usually left their old boats on the beach to break up in the winter gales, or use them for firewood. The Scottish Fisheries Museum at Anstruther has a few original boats and even has two in commission but as far as I know not one original Loch Fyne Skiff remains in its original state. A replica Scoth Niseach, *An Sulaire* was built in Lewis by John Murdo McLeod in 1998 and is a fine example of traditional boat building skills.

    The traditional powered Scottish fishing boat was a direct development of the skiff. The canoe stern was retained but with an inboard rudder and many boats had varnished hulls. These were handsome boats which were used for all types of fishing on the West Coast reaching the peak of development in the fifties and sixties, later to be replaced by the more functional but uglier boats we see today. At that time there were many fishing boat builders turning out wooden fishing boats in large numbers. Noble of Girvan was one such yard where my father had *Tunnag* built on fishing boat lines. There were several important yards on the East Coast including Noble of Fraserburgh and the well known businesses of Herd and McKenzie and Jones in Buckie. It was noticeable to those of us who remember the old boats, how the crews took a pride in them. They never went home without clearing up the decks and stowing or drying their nets and gear. Paint and varnish work were kept in good condition and the boats were usually well maintained. At fishing ports today, many of the boats are seem unkempt, although no doubt functional and there seems to be a lack of pride in their appearance, probably due to general discouragement amongst the ever dwindling number of fishermen due to government policies. I apologise in advance to any fisherman who disagrees with me.

    For those interested in maritime history and historic boats, there are a few locations in Scotland where some vessels have been preserved. The Scottish Maritime Museum in Irvine has some interesting vessels in its collection including one of the oldest William Fife yachts in existence. The *Vagrant* is a "plank on edge" cutter built in 1884. So named because she was built at a time when extremely narrow beam was fashionable. With a beam only 5 feet on an overall length of 22 feet with a 15 foot bowsprit, she is a rarity today and interesting historically. The museum is in the process of organising her complete restoration. The "puffer" *Spartan* has recently been restored at Irvine and the *Carola* is a fine example of a Victorian steam yacht. The barque *Carrick* lies ashore at Irvine awaiting new owners who plan to restore her to her former glory. Originally the *City of Adelaide* she was built for the Australian wool and passenger trade. After world war two she became the headquarters of the R.N.V.R. Club and was moored on the Clyde in the centre of Glasgow for many years. Sadly the ship sank at her berth in the eighties due to debris collecting below her bottom and damaging the hull at low tide, but was eventually the club presented her to the Scottish Maritime Museum for restoration. Unfortunately the museum has been unable to raise the necessary funds for this project but I hope her future will soon be secured.

I have already mentioned the Scottish Fisheries Museum in Anstruther which traces the history of Scottish fishing from its earliest beginnings to the present day. The museum owns the *Reaper* which is a perfectly restored Fifie and can sometimes be seen under sail. They also have one of the last of the huge Zulus in their shed, which although in damaged condition shows clearly how these vessels were constructed. The museum has a workshop where small boat repairs are carried out in view of visitors.

In Glasgow we have the *Glenlee* mentioned earlier, one of the last Clydebuilt sailing ships left in the world. She is now museum ship and can be visited. There is a branch of the Scottish Maritime Museum at Braehead near Renfrew who also own the Denny Test Tank in Dumbarton. The Glasgow Transport Museum has a wonderful collection of ship models which are due to be re-housed in a new museum over the next few years and the Aberdeen Maritime Museum is very interesting with models and exhibits featuring all types of ships from clippers to oil rigs.

On the subject of Tall Ships, At the various Tall Ships Races I have attended most European maritime nations are represented by one of more of their own large sailing vessels. Scotland, with the exception of *Jean de la Lune* a small brigantine converted from a French fishing boat and ably handled and chartered by her owner/skipper John Reid. I have had a "bee in my bonnet" about this for years. It seems a great shame that Scotland with all her maritime and shipbuilding history has no national sailing ship. Small countries like Norway, Denmark and the Netherlands all have such ships and the Tall Ships Races have finished or started at several Scottish ports over the last few years. At these events the interest by the general public is immense and huge crowds gather to see and go aboard the ships. Surely as a nation we can find the means to have a tall ship of our own. Such a vessel could be operated by a company for promotional purposes or perhaps a city such as Glasgow or Edinburgh could have a city ship, examples from elsewhere being the *Stad Amsterdam* which represents the city of Amsterdam or the *Pride of Baltimore* which promotes Baltimore in the U.S.A. wherever she goes. I think that if properly promoted and organised a Scottish Tall Ship project could be successful and provide our young people with the opportunity of a lifetime. There have been a few attempts to start such a project but until now there has been little support from the bodies which could make this happen. Perhaps this will change in the future, those of us who are interested can only hope for a change in attitudes.

Sails and sun aboard Macaria

Chapter 10 - Epilogue

There you have it. If you have reached this far, you will understand my interest in ships and the sea. I hope you have enjoyed my ramblings and found my modest adventures interesting. Life is full of surprises and many things have turned out different from what was commonly assumed. I like to look back at previous predictions of the future years. I recently read an article in an old yachting magazine from the sixties which predicted that by the 21st Century yachts would be almost entirely made on plastic – *true!* That they would all have inflatable sails – *false!* That yacht engines would be so small and quiet that you would hardly hear them running – *partly true!* That yachts would become more alike and less individual – *certainly true!* That yachts would be much smaller that hitherto – *false,* on the last point, there are more large yachts afloat today than ever before. That their numbers would increase – *true* and that we would all tie up in special harbours rather than conventional moorings – *true.* That traditional boat building and sailing skills would completely die out and be forgotten – *false!* What was not predicted was that yachts would be built to traditional designs such as Falmouth workboats or Pilot Cutters in glassfibre, - or that yachts of over 100 years old would be restored and raced again. Please do not think I am against all modern innovations. The vast improvements in navigational aids, new materials and building methods like synthetic sails and rope as well as the many other uses of plastics and adhesives including much improved yachting clothing have all greatly benefited the sport. It is only the fact that so many modern yachts just like modern cars lack character and are so similar. Why are so many white? Why not more coloured hulls or coloured sails? Yachtsmen used to be strongly individual, why have they become so alike? Perhaps it is just the way we are today. What is true is that many more people enjoy sailing in all its forms now than in the past, and everywhere you go around the coast there are yachts to be seen in harbours or at moorings.

Who could have imagined that the "J" Class would be revived, or that the America's Cup Jubilee regatta would be held at Cowes for so many classic yachts including 37 12 metre yachts? The revival in traditional yachts and sailing ships was certainly not predicted in my youth. It is heartening for me and others who love old boats to see all the activity today and it is particularly pleasing to see that it is not just the old timers but large numbers of young people of all nationalities are learning the skills required to build, maintain and sail these vessels. Anyway there is nothing new under the sun; many so called innovations have been used for years, for example. Fin and bulb keels are not as modern as many think but used in extreme racing boats 100 years ago. Roller furling headsails - the Wykham Martin furling gear designed in the early years of the 20th century was the prototype for modern systems. Sheet and halyard winches of various types were used in many vessels from Thames barges to square riggers many years before they became common on yachts. Unstayed masts were common in fishing skiffs such as the Scottish east coast Zulus which had vast dipping lugsails supported by the halyard on the weather side, before any of the yachting experiments with unstayed masts which seem to have been largely abandoned now.

These are just a few thoughts about the scene today. I will finish now with a few quotes from the past and wish you fair winds and a safe landfall wherever you go.

On – Yachting Etiquette!

If you wear a white top cap,
You must always say yacht and never say Yat!

If you must wear your yachting cap on the steamer to Rothesay, don't be surprised or annoyed when old ladies ask you for a timetable or hand you their ticket when going ashore

On – Weather Forecasting!

Glass steady if held in both hands!

If you can see Arran it's going to rain, if you can't see Arran it's raining,!

When the moon is roon' and fair, the fishes swim from Troon to Ayr
When the moon is fair and roon' the fishes swim from Ayr to Troon!

On – Local Knowledge!

Yachtsman anchored in remote highland anchorage on a Sunday went ashore to a farm for milk. On politely asking the farmer's wife she retorted "You will get no milk from me; you with your sails a flap, flap, flapping on the Sabbath!"

On – Why do we do it?

Sailing – The fine art of getting wet and becoming sick while slowly going nowhere at great expense!

Remember and repeat over and over when its blowing force 8 and you're stormbound in a remote West Coast anchorage – "A yacht is a vessel built for pleasure, A yacht is a vessel built for pleasure!!!"

He who goes to sea for pleasure would gladly go to hell for a pastime!

On – Crewing

Always remember to put things back where you found them and always belay a line on the same pin or cleat where it was before you touched it

It may not be your way, or even the best way but if it's the Skipper's way, do it his way.

On – Fitting Out

What is this I see before mine eyes?
A form in stained and tattered dungarees,
A scraper in his hand, one finger clad
In filthy rags, all gory with his blood.
And wherefore doth he toil so frenziedly
On yonder hulk, which seems scarce to bear
The semblance of a ship?

Good stranger that is one of natures anomalies,
A man who toils and sweats for many months
To undergo discomforts on the sea,
And miserable in his hours of leisure
He, paradoxically, deems it pleasure.

Appendix 1 - Details of yachts

DETAILS OF YACHTS IN ALPHABETICAL ORDER

Name	Rig	Designer	Builder	Year	Length	Tons TM	Remarks
Adastra X	8m Cruiser Racer	McGruer	Woodnut	1954	41.8	10	
Adix	3 Mast Schooner	A Holgate	Astilloros de Palma	1983	174.0	N/K	Ex Jessica, ex Schooner XXXX
Aeolian	Bermudan Yawl	Robert Clark	Minnow Yacht Co	1953	40.0	11	Wrecked
Aline	Bermudan Sloop	A Mylne	A Malcolm	1909	42.4	11	
Altair	Gaff Schooner	W Fife III	Fife of Fairlie	1931	107.8	161	
Altricia	8m Cruiser Racer	McGruer	McGruer	1965	41.8	12	
America II	Gaff Schooner	N/K	Goudy & Stephens	1967	130.0	N/K	Replic of schooner America
Arcturus	Bermudan Yawl	E A Gardner	Williams & Parkinson	1935	43.5	19	Ex The Cruiser
Astra	Int 23 Metre Cutter	C Nicholson	Camper & Nicholson	1928	115.0	164	
Atlantic	3 Mast Schooner	H J Gielow	Bethlehem S B Corp	1903	120.0	198	
Australia II	Int 12 Metre Sloop	Ben Lexcen	N/K	1982	65.3	33	
Ayrshire Lass	Gaff Cutter	W Fife II	Fife of Fairlie	1887	24.0	4	
Belle Aventure	Bermudan Yawl	W Fife III	Fife of Fairlie	1929	84.6	94	Ex Eileen
Bernera	Scottish Islander	A Mylne	McGruer	1929	28.2	5	
Boomerang	Brittany Class	Laurent Giles	H McLean	1955	33.5	8	
Camilla of Rhu	8m Cruiser Racer	McGruer	McGruer	1959	42.0	11	
Candida	Int 23 Metre Cutter	C Nicholson	Camper & Nicholson	1929	117.1	174	
Carron II	Int 8 Metre Sloop	W Fife III	Fife of Fairlie	1934	48.0	11	
Catriona	Gareloch OD	McGruer	McGruer	1924	24.0	4	
Celaeno	Bermudan Sloop	McGruer	McGruer	1951	30.3	8	
Cerigo	Int 12 Metre Sloop	W Fife III	Fife of Fairlie	1926	66.0	33	Ex Roska
Charm of Rhu II	Bermudan Ketch	A Mylne	Bute Slip Dock	1930	74.7	62	
Cintra	Int 12 M Gaff Cutter	W Fife III	Fife of Fairlie	1909	61.9	26	
Circe	Int 6 Metre Sloop	David Boyd	Alex Robertson	1937	38.6	5	
Clio	Bermudan Sloop	W Fife III	Fife of Fairlie	1906	41.0	16	
Coigach	Bermudan Yawl	McGruer	McGruer	1963	43.2	17	
Columbia	Int 12 Metre Sloop	S & Stephens	Nevins Yacht Yard	1958	69.4	33	
Creole	3 Mast Schooner	C Nicholson	Camper & Nicholson	1927	399.2	699	

Name	Rig	Designer	Builder	Year	Length	Tons TM	Remarks
Cruinaig III	Bermudan Ketch	W Campbell	Dickie of Tarbert	1936	63.7	47	
Deb	Bermudan Sloop	S & Stephens	McGruer	1965	39.8	16	
Debbie	8m Cruiser Racer	McGruer	McGruer	1966	41.8	12	
Dirk II	Gaff Yawl	W Fife III	E H Arp, Laboe	1921	41.0	17	Bermudan rigged when on the Clyde
Dochas	Bermudan Sloop	McGruer	McGruer	1962	29.8	8	
Dyarchy	Gaff Cutter	Laurent Giles	S Truedsson	1939	46.5	27	
Earraid	Motor Ketch	G L Watson	Morris & Lorimer	1948	42.0	27	
Eileen	Bermudan Cutter	W Fife III	Fife of Fairlie	1935	60.4	33	Originally yawl being restored
Eilidh	Bermudan Cutter	A Milne	Dickie of Bangor	1931	58.3	30	
Eleonora	Gaff Schooner	Gaastmeer	Gaastmeer	2002	136.0	323	Replica of schooner Westward
Elfin of Lorne	Bermudan Sloop	McGruer	McGruer	1964	29.0	7	
Elise	Gaff Schooner	W Fife III	Fife of Fairlie	1911	65.0	39	
Elona	Bermudan Yawl	McGruer	McGruer	1962	40.2	13	
Endeavour 1	J Class Cutter	C Nicholson	Camper & Nicholson	1934	129.7	205	
Endeavour II	J Class Cutter	C Nicholson	Camper & Nicholson	1936	135.8	228	
Esteril	Gaff Int 8 Metre	Leon Sebille	Chantiers Leon Sebille	1912	N/K	N/K	
Fabella	Bermudan Ketch	Laurent Giles	Groves & Gutteridge	1961	52.8	35	
Feolinn	8m Cruiser Racer	McGruer	McGruer	1961	42.0	12	
Finvola	Int 6 m Sloop	W Fife III	Fife of Fairlie	1925	35.9	5	
Fionnuala	8m Cruiser Racer	McGruer	McGruer	1961	42.0	13	Ex Debbie
Flica II	Int 12 Metre Sloop	Laurent Giles	Fife of Fairlie	1938	66.7	33	
Flicka	Fisksatra 41	Knut Reimers	Fisksatra Varv	1982	41.0	N/K	
Freedom	Int 12 Metre Sloop	S & Stephens	Minneford Yacht Yard	1979	62.3	32	
Fulmar	Int 8 Metre Sloop	W Fife III	Fife of Fairlie	1930	48.5	13	
Fynelyne	Gaff Yawl	D Raeburn	Clyde Classics	1992	34.0	12	
Gabrielle III	Bermudan Sloop	S & Stephens	McGruer	1967	53.0	24	
Gigi of Clynder	8m C/R Yawl	J McGruer	McGruer	1960	41.9	13	
Glenafton	Bermudan Ketch	A Milne	Bute Slip Dock	1967	59.2	50	
Gosling	Int 6 Metre Sloop	S & Stephens	McGruer	1971	33.1	5	
Griselda	Bermudan Yawl	W Fife III	Fife of Fairlie	1906	88.0	80	Ex Thelma IV, ex Vida VI, ex Rose

Name	Rig	Designer	Builder	Year	Length	Tons TM	Remarks
Gunna	Bermudan Ketch	McGruer	McGruer	1946	48.0	21	
Hattasoo	17/19 Gaff Sloop	W Fife III	Fife of Fairlie	1894	19.0	3	
Helen	Int 8m Sloop	Glen Coats	Bute Slip Dock	1936	47.0	10	
Hirta	Gaff Pilot Cutter	J Slade	J Slade	1911	46.0	33	Ex Cornubia
Hispania	Int 15m Gaff Cutter	W Fife III	Astilleros Karrpard	1909	76.2	50	Undergoing restoration
If	Int 8m Sloop	Bjarne Aas	Bjarne Aas	1930	48.8	12	Based at Aldeburgh Sussex
Ilderim	Int 8m Sloop	Tore Holm	Abrahamsson	1936	50.4	12	Formerly Christina of Cascais
Innismara	Int 8m Sloop	J McGruer	McGruer	1963	41.5	12	
Intrepid	Int 12 Metre Sloop	S & Stephens	Minneford Yacht Yard	1967	64.6	33	
Iolaire	Bermudan Ketch	Harris Bros	Harris Bros	1905	45.5	17	
Iroquois	Int 8m Sloop	S & Stephens	Minneford Yacht Yard	1968	43.5	10	
Iskareen	Int 8m Sloop	S & Stephens	Stockholms Batb	1939	48.8	11	Briefly named Cheetah
Ivanhoe	Bermudan Sloop	C A Nicholson	Moody & Son	1959	35.0	9	
Jap	Gaff Sloop	W Fife III	Carrigaloe	1897	30.0	6	
Josephine IV	Int 8m Sloop	J McGruer	Moody & Son	1953	39.1	10	Wrecked 1969
June	Int 8m Sloop	J Anker	Anker & Jensen	1929	48.9	13	Once owned by Errol Flynn
Karenita	Bermudan Ketch	N/K	N/K	1923	N/K	N/K	
Kentra	Gaff Ketch	W Fife III	Fife of Fairlie	1923	82.3	87	
Kyla II	Bermudan Sloop	J McGruer	McGruer	1974	38.3	16	
Lady Anne	Int 15m Gaff Cutter	W Fife III	Fife of Fairlie	1912	72.0	51	
Lelantina	Gaff Schooner	John Alden	Abeking & Rasmussen	1937	74.0	N/K	
Leonora	Gaff Pilot Cutter	Le Marchand	Le Marchand	1928	55.0	38	Ex Marie Fernand
Llygra	Gaff Sloop	A Robertson	Robertsons	1898	31.2	9	Fate unknown
Lola	Bermudan Ketch	J Pain Clark	W King & Sons	1925	38.7	12	
Lulworth	Gaff Cutter	H W White	White Bros	1920	119.5	186	Ex Terpsichore
Lutine	Bermudan Yawl	Laurent Giles	Camper & Nicholson	1952	60.0	35	Formerly Lloyds Yacht Club boat
Macaria	Gaff Yawl	Peter Dickie	Dickie of Tarbert	1922	34.0	9	Now in Essex
Madcap	Gaff Pilot Cutter	Davies & Plain	Davies & Plain	1875	43.2	22	Ex Bristol Channel Pilot Cutter
Madrigal II	Bermudan Sloop	W Fife III	Fairlie Yacht Slip	1951	48.7	18	

Name	Rig	Designer	Builder	Year	Length	Tons TM	Remarks
Magda IV	Gaff Cutter	W Fife III	Jensen-Christiana	1904	46.0	17	
Frenesi of Clynder	Bermudan Yawl	McGruer	McGruer	1961	43.5	17	Ex Marguerita Helena III
Mariette	Gaff Schooner	N Herreshof	Herreschof	1915	109.0	N/K	
Mariquita	Int 19m Gaff Cutter	W Fife III	Fife of Fairlie	1911	95.3	100	Restored by Fairlie Restorations
Margaret	Int 8m Sloop	J Anker	Anker & Jensen	1926	47.2	12	Now in France
Maria-Cha III	Bermudan Ketch	Philipe Briand	N/K	1997	147.5	N/K	
Marie Rose	Motor Yacht	J A McCallum	British Marine	1915	36.0	12	
Mariella	Bermudan Yawl	A Mylne	Fife of Fairlie	1938	79.0	74	
Marina	Int 12m Sloop	A Mylne	Bute Slip Dock	1935	66.0	34	
Melfort	Motor Ketch	G L Watson	McGruer	1947	42.0	25	Wrecked 1946
Merry Dancer	Bermudan Sloop	W Fife III	Fife of Fairlie	1938	51.7	20	Ex Golden Beam
Merrymaid	Gaff Cutter	C Nicholson	Camper & Nicholson	1904	98.5	107	
Mignon	Bermudan Sloop	W Fife III	Fife of Fairlie	1898	28.0	3	
Mikado	Clyde 30 B/Sloop	W Fife III	Fife of Fairlie	1904	35.7	10	
Mingary	Bermudan Ketch	A Milne	Bute Slip Dock	1929	59.4	34	
Mokoia	Bermudan Cutter	A Robb	Stebbings	1948	37.9	10	Built to International 8m rule
Moonbeam	Gaff Cutter	W Fife III	W Fife	1920	95.3	98	
Moonbeam of Fife	Gaff Cutter	W Fife III	W Fife	1903	62.4	67	Originally Moonbeam III
Morning Star	Galway Hooker	N/K	N/K	1890	37.0	N/K	
Muchacha	Frers 39	German Frers	Frers & Cibils	1975	38.6	N/K	
Nahmara	8m Cruiser Racer	McGruer	Bute Slip Dock	1955	40.7	10	
Nan of Clynder	8m Cruiser Racer	McGruer	McGruer	1956	38.8	11	
Nan of Gare	8m Cruiser Racer	McGruer	McGruer	1965	39.8	12	
Nighean Donn	Lugsail skiff	D Munro	D Munro	1921	27.7	7	
Nomad II	Bermudan Ketch	T C Letcher	H Gale, Cowes	1926	52.3	34	
Nordwind	Bermudan Yawl	H Gruber	Burmester	1939	85.0	60	
Northward	Bermudan Sloop	A Mylne	McGruer	1930	50.0	20	Rig altered to ketch 1962
Nymph of Lorne	Bermudan Sloop	McGruer	McGruer	1963	28.7	7	
Opposition	Bermudan Sloop	S & Stephens	Claire Lallow	1971	40.7	20	Ex Morning Cloud
Orana	8m Cruiser Racer	J McGruer	McGruer	1959	42.0	12	
Orani	8m Cruiser Racer	J McGruer	G Cuthbertson	1964	41.0	12	

Name	Rig	Designer	Builder	Year	Length	Tons TM	Remarks
Ortac	Bermudan Cutter	Robert Clark	Morgan Giles	1937	48.2	20	Hamburgischer Verein Seefahrt
Pen Duick	Gaff Cutter	W Fife III	Fife of Fairlie	1898	43.0	16	Ex Yum
Petula	Gaff Yawl	W Fife III	Fife of Fairlie	1899	46.0	18	Sold to "Blondie" Hasler 1946
Pierette	Gaff Sloop	W Fife III	Fife of Fairlie	1899	27.3	4	
Pretty Polly	Gaff Cutter	G L Watson	Alex Robertson	1929	67.0	46	
Puritan	Gaff Schooner	J Alden	Electric Boat Co.	1934	102.7	187	
Ranger	J Class Cutter	John Williams	Danish Yachts	2002	136.0	N/K	
Rinamara	Bermudan Yawl	McGruer	McGruer	1968	47.2	20	
Roland v Bremen	Bermudan Cutter	H Gruber	E Burmester	1938	49.7		Formerly SKWB club yacht
Romeiro	Bermudan Sloop	D Hillyard	D Hillyard	1964	35.0	12	
Ron	Gaff Ketch	J A McCallum	Alex Robertson	1929	59.5	30	
Royono	Bermudan Ketch	John Alden	Herreschoff	1940	72.0	N/K	Once owned by John F Kennedy
Ruach	Gaff Sloop	Paul Gartside	Riverside Products	1983	16.0	2	Ex Mollusc
Sally of Kames	Bermudan Sloop	J McGruer	Bute Slip Dock	1953	33.4	8	
Sgarbh	Motor Ketch	W Campbell	A Adam & Sons	1947	40.0	23	
Sceptre	Int 12m Sloop	David Boyd	Alex Robertson	1968	65.0	35	
Sea Bear	Gaff Ketch	G L Watson	Alex Robertson	1929	40.3	22	
Seabird	Gaff Cutter	W Fife III	Chantier Stagnol	2002	28.0	3	
Seewolf	Bermudan Ketch	W von Hacht	W von Hacht	1937	60.3	34	
Senta	Wishbone Ketch	Max Oertz	Deutsche Werft Kiel	1928	54.0	30	
Seonella	Bermudan Sloop	McGruer	McGruer	1953	34.5	8	Ex Nan of Kames
Severn II od Ardmaleish	Int 8m Sloop	A Mylne	Bute Slip Dock	1934	48.4	11	Sold to Canada
Shamrock V	Int 23m Cutter	C E Nicholson	Camper & Nicholson	1930	120.0	163	
Shenandoah	3 Mast Schooner	T Ferris	Townsend & Downie	1902	157.0	N/K	
Silja	Int 8m Sloop	J Anker	Anker & Jensen	1930	49.0	12	Sold to Finland 1972
Siolta I	Bermudan Cutter	A Mylne	Bute Slip Dock	1936	49.4	18	Ex Gleniffer
Siolta II	Excalibur Sloop	Van de Stadt	Southern Ocean	1966	36.0	11	
Siris	Int 8m Sloop	Morgan Giles	Morgan Giles	1925	48.4	11	Based in S England
Skulmartin	Hustler 30	Holman & Pye	Tyler Boat Co.	1971	30.4	9	
Solway Maid	Bermudan Cutter	W Fife III	Fife of Fairlie	1940	52.6	21	

Name	Rig	Designer	Builder	Year	Length	Tons TM	Remarks
Sonata	Bermudan Sloop	W Fife III	Woodnutt & Co.	1950	52.3	21	
Sonda	8m Cruiser Racer	McGruer	McGruer	1951	39.4	10	
Sovereign	Int 12m Sloop	David Boyd	Alex Robertson	1963	69.2	36	
St. Mary	Bermudan Ketch	Ian Nicolson	Arden Yachts	1961	35.0	N/K	
Starglint	Bermudan Sloop	D Raeburn	Clyde Classics	1992	34.0	N/K	
Stealth	IRC Supermaxi	German Frers	Green Marine	1996	82.0	N/K	
Stornoway	Int 13.5m Yawl	McGruer	Morris & Lorimer	1963	66.7	52	
Sule Skerry	Bermudan Yawl	McGruer	McGruer	1958	43.0	18	
Sunshine	Int 6m Sloop	W Fife III	Fife of Fairlie	1927	35.5	5	
Sibyl of Cumae	Gaff Cutter	W Fife III	Fife of Fairlie	1902	51.7	14	Formerly cutter rigged
Talisker of Lorne	Bermudan Sloop	McGruer	McGruer	1975	34.2	10	
Tem	Gaff Cutter	W Fife III	Hilditch	1897	37.6	9	
The Lady Anne	Int 15m Gaff Cutter	W Fife III	Fife of Fairlie	1912	72.0	51	
The Truant	Int 8m sloop	W Fife III	Fife of Fairlie	1910	41.0	9	
Thendara	Gaff Ketch	A Milne	Stephens of Linthouse	1937	105.0	147	
Thistle	Gaff Sloop	A Mylne	A Malcolm	1909	30.0	4	
Tinkatoo	Bermudan Yawl	C R Holman	Staniland	1960	35.0	10	Ex Trix
Tinto II	8m Cruiser Racer	A MacMillan	Fairlie Yacht Slip	1957	42.7	11	
Todday	Int Dragon	J Anker	McGruer	1948	29.2	N/K	
Tomahawk	Int 12m Sloop	C Nicholson	Camper & Nicholson	1939	69.3	33	
Trefoil of Kames	Bermudan Sloop	A Mylne	Bute Slip Dock	1950	28.2	7	
Tritsch Tratsch 1	Bermudan Sloop	McGruer	McGruer	1971	42.0	17	
Tritsch Tratsch II	Bermudan Sloop	McGruer	McGruer	1973	47.0	29	
Trivia	Int 12m Sloop	C E Nicholson	Camper & Nicholson	1937	70.1	33	
Tuiga	Int 15m Gaff Cutter	W Fife III	Fife of Fairlie	1909	75.0	50	Previously Kismet and Nevada
Tunnag	Motor Ketch	W Campbell	Noble	1953	40.0	23	Now Oronsay
Turid 2	Int 8m Sloop	Bjarne Aas	Bjarne Aas	1939	47.5	11	
Vadura	Bermudan Ketch	A Mylne	A Stephen & Son	1926	91.5	109	
Vagrant	Gaff Cutter	W Fife III	Culzean Yard	1884	22.0	2	
Vagrant II	Int 8m Sloop	W Fife III	Fife of Fairlie	1927	N/K	12	Wrecked in 1980's

Name	Rig	Designer	Builder	Year	Length	Tons TM	Remarks
Vim	Int 12m Sloop	S & Stephens	Henry B Nevins	1939	69.6	35	
Viola	Gaff Cutter	W Fife III	Fife of Fairlie	1908	41.0	12	
Wanderer III	Bermudan Sloop	Laurent Giles	W King Ltd	1952	30.3	8	
Westward of Clynder	Bermudan Yawl	McGruer	McGruer	1960	43.5	17	
Wind of Clynder	Bermudan Sloop	McGruer	McGruer	1964	29.3	8	
Wye	Int 8m Sloop	C Nicholson	Camper & Nicholson	1935	48.6	11	Sold to Sweden 1973
Zulu	Bermudan Sloop	Laurent Giles	Morris & Lorimer	1957	47.5	19	Now Cetawago

The data shown has been gathered from various sources, the author cannot guaratee accuracy

N/K indicates information not known to author

Appendix 2 - Details of tall ships

DETAILS OF TALL SHIPS IN ALPHABETICAL ORDER

Name	Rig	Nationality	Year	Length	Remarks
Alexander von Humboldt	3 Mast Barque	German	1906	177.5	Former lightship
Asgard II	Brigantine	Irish	1981	88.0	
Astrid	Brig	Netherlands	1918	109.0	
Carrick	3 mast Barque	U.K.	1864	180.0	Ex City of Adelaide
Christian Radich	3 Mast Ship	Norwegian	1937	205.0	
Cisne Branca	3 Mast Ship	Brazil	1999	214.0	Sister Ship to Stad Amsterdam
Cuauhtemoc	3 Mast barque	Mexican	1982	258.0	Mexican Navy Training Vessel
Danmark	3 Mast Ship	Danish	1933	213.0	
Dar Mlojesy	3 Mast Ship	Poland	1982	310.0	Sister Ship to Mir
Druzhba	3 Mast Ship	Russian	N/K	310.0	Sister Ship to Mir
Eagle	3 Mast Barque	U.S.A.	1936	266.0	U.S. Coastguard Vessel
Europa	3 Mast Barque	Netherlands	1911	149.0	Former lightship
Eye of the Wind	Brigantine	Danish	1911	106.0	Ex Merry
Falkan	2 Mast Schooner	Swedish	1947	113.0	
Frederyk Chopin	Brig	Polish	1990	144.0	
Georg Stage	3 Mast Ship	Danish	1934	138.0	
Gladan	2 Mast Schooner	Swedish	1947	113.0	
Glenlee	3 Mast Barque	U.K.	1896	233.0	Ex Islamount, ex Galatea
Gorch Fock 1	3 Mast Barque	German	1933	241.0	Ex Tovarisch
Gorch Fock 2	3 Mast Barque	German	1958	266.0	German Navy Training Vessel
Gunilla	3 Mast Barque	Swedish	1940	138.0	
Jean de la Lune	Brigantine	U.K.	1957	81.0	
Kershones	3 Mast Ship	Ukraine	1989	310.0	Sister Ship to Mir
Kruzenstern	4 Mast Barque	Russian	1926	375.0	Ex Padua

157

Name	Rig	Nationality	Year	Length	Remarks
Libertad	3 Mast Ship	Argentina	1956	300.0	Argentinian Navy Training Ship
Lord Nelson	3 Mast Barque	U.K.	1985	140.0	Specially equipped for disabled people
Malcolm Miller	Topsail Schooner	Formerly U.K.	1968	135.0	
Matthew	Caravel Barque	U.K.	1976	78.0	Replica of John Cabot's Caravel
Mir	3 Mast Ship	Russian	1987	310.0	
Moshulu	4 Mast Barque	U.S.A.	1904	360.0	Ex Kurt, Formerly in Erikson Fleet
Naziezda	3 Mast Ship	Russian	N/K	310.0	Sister Ship to Mir
Osterschelde	3 M T/Sail Schooner	Netherlands	1918	133.0	
Pallada	3 Mast Ship	Russian	N/K	310.0	Sister Ship to Mir
Pallinuro	Barquentine	Italian	1934	193.0	Italian Navy Training Vessel
Pogoria	Barquentine	Poland	1980	135.0	
Pride of Baltimore	2 M T/Sail Schooner	U.S.A.	1977	90.0	Replica Baltimore Clipper
Prince William	Brig	U.K.	2002	194.0	S.T.A. Training Vessel
Roald Admundsen	Brig	Germany	1952	138.0	
Royal Clipper	5 mast ship	U.K.	2000	439.0	Sailing cruise ship, world's largest sailing vessel
Royalist	Brig	U.K.	1971	76.5	Sea Cadets Training Vessel
Sagres	3 Mast Barque	Portugal	1937	267.0	Portugese Navy Training Vessel
Sedov	4 Mast Barque	Russian	1921	385.0	Ex Magdelene Vinnen Ex Kommodore Johnston
Shabab Oman	3 Mast Barquentine	Oman	1971	N/K	Ex Captain Scott
Sir Winston Churchill	Topsail Schooner	Formerly U.K.	1966	135.0	
Soren Larsen	Brigantine	U.K.	1949	104.0	
Sorlandet	3 Mast Ship	Norwegian	1928	186.0	
Stad Amsterdam	3 Mast Ship	Netherlands	2000	214.0	Built on Clipper Ship lines
Statsraad Lehmkuhl	3 Mast Barque	Norwegian	1914	259.0	

Name	Rig	Nationality	Year	Length	Remarks
Stavros Niarchos	Brig	U.K.	2001	194.0	S.T.A. Training Vessel
Swan van Makkum	Brigantine	Netherlands	1993	163.0	World's Largest Brigantine
Tenacious	3 Mast Barque	U.K.	2001	214.0	Specially equipped for disabled people

The data shown has been gathered from various sources, the author cannot guaratee accuracy

N/K indicates information not known to author

Appendix 3 - Sailing Vessel Rigs

Appendix 4 - Clyde Cruising Club Song

If you cruise on the Clyde.
And you wish to decide
On the Club that will suit you the best;
If you're feeing in doubt
With so many about,
There is one I should like to suggest:
This Club doesn't mind for the build of your craft,
And puts no restriction on beam or on draft,
So whether your boat is a barge or a yacht.
The Clyde Cruising Club is the best of the lot.

Chorus
C.C.C., all impartial observers agree
That the Club is still growing and growing,
But where it will stop there's no knowing;
C.C.C., you've an artistocratic burgee,
And is puts in the shade any flag ever made
Does the C.C.C.

You will find it amusing
To watch while you're cruising
The pride of each boy in his boat:
Though as old as the Ark
He is sure to remark,
"There's nothing to touch her afloat".
His mainsail is frequently mildewed and black.
With a patch at the clew and a tear at the tack,
And his jib has a belly and flaps at the leach,
Yet he swears that his boat is a perfect wee peach.

Chorus
C.C.C., though your boats are of every degree,
Though some may be splendidly fitted –
Some leak and the owners are pitied;
C.C.C., if at Rothesay you happen to be,
There's a fellow, they say, pumping boats half the day
For the C.C.C.

So when once you're a member,
From May to September
You'll find us in every port;
In our burgee you see,
You may take it from me
You'll find camaradie is our forte.
Every species of cruiser this Club seem to suit,
From the Commodore down to the latest recruit;
We are greatly admired when we sail down the Clyde,
But observe us when fostering our social side.

Chorus
C.C.C., you're the very best Club that could be,
At this dinner I feel I'm in clover,
But what shall I think when it's over?
C.C.C., though your motto is camaradie,
When they put me to bed with a Colintraive head
We shall C.C.C.

This is the original version of the club song which was composed by Murray Blair and sung for the first time at the Club's first Annual Dinner at the Charing Cross Hotel in Glasgow on 2nd December 1910

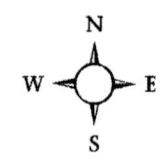

Appendix 5 - The Seaman's Language, a glossary

Aback	Wind on wrong side of sail
Abaft	Behind or aft of
Abeam	At right angles to centreline of vessel
About	To move vessel from one tack to the other
Aft	Behind, the hinder part of a vessel
Aground	When a vessel is grounded on the sea bottom
Ahead	Directly in front of the vessel
Aloft	Above deck level, in the rigging
Amidships	The centre section of a vessel
Astern	Directly behind the vessel
Avast	Stop, cease
Aweigh	When anchor is clear of the bottom
Backstay	Standing rigging to support the mast from aft
Baggywrinkle	Material fixed to stays to protect sails from chafe
Bail	To remove water from inside a boat with a container
Ballast	Weights placed inside a vessel for trimming
Barque	Three or more mast vessel square rigged on all but after mast
Barquentine	Three or more mast vessel square rigged on foremast only
Batten	Lightwood or plastic inserts to control sail shape
Beam	The width of a vessel at her widest part
Bear away	To steer the ship away from the prevailing wind
Beating	To sail to windward
Bearing	Direction of ship or object in relation to compass
Beaufort	Numerical scale of wind force 0-12
Becket	Loop in rope or end fixture on bloc
Belay	To secure rope on cleat or belaying pin
Belaying Pin	Metal or wood pin used to hold rope secure
Bend	Type of knot or to secure with rope
Bells	Time aboard ship announced by bell strokes
Bermudan	Fore and aft rig with triangular mainsail
Berth	Bed for sleeping aboard ship or ship's place in harbour

Bight	Unknotted loop in a rope
Bilge	Curve of vessel's underbody or bottom interior of vessel
Binnacle	Housing for ship's compass
Bitts	Strong posts at bow to hold anchor or mooring cables
Block	Wood, metal or plastic pulley for rope or wire rigging
Bobstay	Wire or chain to prevent bowsprit from lifting
Bollard	Strong deck fitting to secure mooring lines
Boot Top	Painted waterline between topsides and bottom
Bottle Screw	Screw adjuster for standing rigging, see also rigging screw
Bow	Forward end of vessel
Bower	Main anchor
Bowsprit	Spar projecting from bow to support headsails
Brace	Ropes from yards to control square sails
Brail	Ropes to furl fore and aft sails
Brig	Two mast vessel with square sails on both masts
Brigantine	Two mast vessel with square sails on foremast only
Brightwork	Varnished wood finish
Broach	When ship swings uncontrollably broadside to wind and sea
Bulkhead	Upright "walls" or partitions inside hull
Bullseye	Hardwood eye for leading rope through
Bullwarks	Sides of a vessel above deck level
Bumkin	As bowsprit but at the stern
Bunk	Seagoing bed for crew to sleep in
Buntline	Ropes to furl square sails from the deck
Buoy	Metal or plastic float for navigation or mooring
Burgee	Triangular or swallow tail flag denoting yacht club
By the lee	Sailing with the wind aft but on the lee side
Cable	Anchor chain or rope, also distance measurement
Canoe Stern	Pointed stern as in a canoe
Cant	To turn around
Capstan	Mechanical device for hauling a rope or cable
Captain	Senior officer, first in command
Carvel	Boatbuilding method with smooth planking
Cast Off	To loosen ropes holding vessel to land
Catamaran	Vessel with twin hulls
Cathead	Fitting or crane to lift anchor for stowage
Caulking	Making watertight by packing material into seams
Centreboard	Fin of wood or metal to diminish leeway
Chafe	To rub causing damage to sails or rope

Chain Plate	Fittings at side of ship to hold stays supporting mast
Chart	Nautical map
Chronometer	Accurate clock used for navigation
Cleat	A shaped fitting to secure ropes
Clew	Corner of sail where sheet is attached
Clewline	Line to haul squaresail clew up to yard
Clinker	Boatbuilding method with overlapping planks
Clipper	Fast square rigged sailing vessel
Clipper Bow	Concave shaped bow as in clipper ships, see also fiddle bow
Close Hauled	Sailing close to the wind
Coach Roof	Raised cabin top
Coaming	Side of cockpit, coachroof or hatch above deck level
Cockpit	Well where helmsman and crew work and sit
Companion	Ladder or stairway to interior of vessel
Compass	Navigational instrument showing direction of North
Composite	Construction method using metal frames with wood planking
Counter	Stern extending aft of rudder stock
Course (1)	Direction of ships' track
Course (2)	Lowest square sail on any mast except aftermost
Cradle	Support frame for boat out of water
Cranse Iron	Metal fitting at bowsprit end
Cringle	Metal eye sewn into a sail
Crossjack	Lowest square sail on aftermost mast
Cro'jack	Abbreviation for Crossjack
Crosstrees	Struts fitted on mast to spread stays (see also spreader)
Crutch	Support for boom or fitting to hold oars in rowing position
Cutter	Single mast vessel with more than one headsail
Dacron	Synthetic sailcloth
Davit	Crane for lifting ships boats
Deadeye	Wooden fitting with holes for tensioning rigging
Deadlight	Metal cover to protect glass of porthole
Derrick	Crane for handling cargo
Deviation	Compass error caused by proximity of iron
Dinghy	Small open boat, see also tender
Dipping Lug	Lugsail that must be lowered when tacking
Displacement	Weight of a vessel in tons
Doghouse	Raised cabin top over coachroof
Downhaul	Line to pull down a sail or spar

Drag	Insecure anchor, not holding on sea bottom
Draught	Depth of hull underwater
Draw	To fill with wind (sails)
Dress	To dress a mast with string of flags
Ease	To slacken a rope
Ebb	Falling tide
Echo Sounder	Instrument to measure depth of water
Eddy	Circular movement of tidal water
Ensign	National flag
Fairlead	Fitting to guide and direct a rope
Fairway	Navigable channel
Fall	Hauling part of a rope or rope purchase on davits
Fathom	Nautical measurement of 6 feet
Fender	Cushion to prevent damage to hull
Fend off	To push vessel off land or other vessel
Fetch	To achieve course for destination
Fid	Tapered wooden tool for rope splicing
Fiddle Block	Block with sheaves above each other
Fiddle Bow	Concave shaped bow, see also clipper bow
Fiddles	Wood strips to secure objects on table at sea
Fife Rail	Wooden rail fitted on deck round a mast for belaying pins
Fifie	Scottish east coast sailing fishing boat
Fisherman	Staysail set between the masts of a schooner
Fit Out	To overhaul and prepare a vessel for sea
Fix	To find a ship's position by taking bearings
Flake down	To lay out ropes for free running
Flare (1)	Outward curve of bow at side of ship
Flare (2)	Pyrotechnic distress signal
Floor	Transverse member joining frames to keel
Fluke	Point of an anchor
Foot	Lower edge of a sail
Footropes	Ropes or wires fixed below a yard for crew to stand on
Fore	Forward, opposite of aft
Forecastle	Accomodation below foredeck
Foc'sle	Abbreviation of Forecastle
Forefoot	Junction of stem and keel
Forepeak	The foremast part of a vessel below deck
Foresail	Fore and aft sail set on schooner's foremast
Frame	Ribs of vessel, usually timber or steel
Free	Opposite of close hauled

Freeboard	Height of vessels side above waterline
Full & Bye	As close hauled
Gabbart	Obsolete Scottish cargo carrying sailing boat
Gaff	Spar fixed to head of fore and aft sail
Gaff Jaws	Fitting on inboard end of gaff to allow it slide on mast
Gaff Rig	Fore and aft rig with quadrilateral sail
Gale	Wind force 8 on Beaufort scale
Galley	Ship's kitchen
Gallows	Fitting to support boom when not in use
Galvanised	Zinc coating on steel to prevent corrosion
Gammon Iron	Ring fitting at stem to hold bowsprit
Garboard	Planks next to the keel
Gaskets	Ropes or canvas straps to tie sails when furled also tiers
Genoa	Large overlapping headsail
Gimbals	Device to hold items level at sea e.g. cooker, compass etc.
Gipsy	Wheel on windlass to hold chain links
Gollywobbler	Large light weather fisherman's staysail on schooner rig
Gooseneck	Universal joint fitting for holding spar to mast
G.P.S.	Global positioning system
G.R.P.	Glass reinforced plastic, glassfibre or fibreglass
Grating	Wooden framework with square holes
Gripes	Canvas or webbing bands to hold down boats stowed on deck
Grommet	Rope ring
Guard Rail	Railings round vessel to prevent crew from falling overboard
Gudgeon	Eye fittings on sternpost to hold rudder pintles
Gunter Rig	Triangular mainsail supported by a yard
Gunwale	Upper edge of a boat's side
Guy	Controlling rope to end of a spar e.g. spinnaker guy
Gybe	To bring the wind from one quarter to the other when aft
Halyard	Rope or wire for hoisting sail or flag
Hand	To take in or stow a sail
Handy Billy	Small block and tackle purchase for occasional use
Hanks	Clips or rings to hold foresails to stays
Harden in	To haul in a sheet to flatten a sail
Hard Down	Putting helm as far as possible to leeward
Hard Up	Putting helm as far as possible to windward
Haul	To pull
Hawse Pipe	Hole through which anchor cable runs

Hawser	Large mooring cable of rope or wire
Head	Top edge or top corner of a sail
Headboard	Triangular board sewn into head of a bermudan mainsail
Heads	Sea Toilet
Headsail	Sail set forward of foremast
Headway	Forward movement of vessel
Heave To	To hold a vessel almost stationary under sail
Heaving Line	Light rope attached to hawser to facilitate throwing
Heel	Inclination of a vessel sideways or lower end of a mast
Helm	Steering wheel or tiller to control rudder
Hemp	Natural fibre for traditional rope making
Highfield lever	Mechanical lever device to tension or release rigging
High Water	High tide
Hitch	Knot
Hogged	When sheer line becomes distorted due to strain
Hoist	To haul aloft or pull up
Holy Stone	Stone block used to scour decks
Hood End	Ends of planks where they join stem or sternpost
Hoops	Wooden rings to hold gaff sail close to mast
Horse	Metal bar across deck for sheet block to slide on
Hounds	Supports on a mast to hold lower standing rigging
Hull	Body of a vessel excluding masts and rigging
Hurricane	Force 12 on the Beaufort scale
In	One is said to be "in" a vessel not "on" her
Irons	When vessel is head to wind with no steerage way
Jackstay	Rod or wire on yard to hold head of squaresail
Jackyard	Spar attached to topsail to extend foot beyond the gaff
Jib	Foremost headsail
Jib Boom	Spar attached to bowsprit to extend its length
Jib Topsail	Light weather jib set on topmast stay
Jigger	Aftermost mast on 4 masted rig
Jumper Stay	Stay on foreside of mast to support upper part
Jury Rig	Makeshift rig used in emergency
Kedge	Small anchor
Keel	Lowest part of a vessel
Ketch	Two mast fore and aft vessel with mizzen forward of rudder
Kicking Strap	Tackle or mechanical device to hold boom down
King Plank	Centre line deck plank
Knee	Bracket of wood or metal to strengthen hull inside the vessel

Knot	Nautical mile per hour
Lanyard	Lashing for any purpose also for setting up deadeye rigging
Lash	To tie down
Latitude	Position north or south of the equator expressed in degrees
Lay	The way a rope of constructed e.g. left or right hand lay
Lay Up	To store a vessel when out of commission
Lazyjack	Ropes fixed to control sails when lowering
L.B.P.	Length between perpendiculars
Launch	To put vessel in the water also small motor tender
Leach	After edge of fore and aft sail, or vertical edge of square sail
Lead	Lead weight used with line to measure depth of water
Leader	Rope used to hold topsail close to mast in gaff rig
Lee	Opposite side from wind direction
Leeboard	Pivoted boards on vessel's side to provide lateral resistance
Lee Helm	When vessel has a tendency to fall off the wind
Lee Shore	Coastline with wind blowing directly onto shore
Leeway	Sideways movement of vessel through the water
Leg	Support for hull when out of the water
Lifeline	Safety line for crew
Lignum Vitae	Extremely hard wood used for deadeyes, bulls eyes etc.
Limber Holes	Holes in floors to allow flow of bilge water
Lines	Drawings of a vessel showing hull shape also light ropes
List	Inclination of a vessel to one side
L.O.A.	Length over all, extreme length of hull excluding spars
L.O.D.	Length on deck, (recent expression for L.O.A.)
Locker	Cupboard or store
Log	Instrument to measure ship's speed and distance run
Log Book	Day to day record of ship's position and events aboard
Longitude	Position east or west of Greenwich expressed in degrees
Low Water	Low tide
Lubber Line	Line on compass to show ship's head
Luff	Forward edge of sail also to turn vessel to windward
Lugsail	Quadrilateral fore and aft sail with a yard crossing the mast
L.W.L.	Load waterline, measurement of hull length at waterline
Mainsail	Fore and aft sail set on aft side of mainmast
Make Fast	To secure

Man Rope	Rope on gangway to assist boarding
Manila	Natural fibre for traditional rope making
Marline	Tarred twine for rigging work
Marline Spike	Tapered steel tool for working with rope e.g. splicing
Mast	Vertical spar to hold sails and rigging
Mast Step	Socket to support heel or foot of mast
Masthead	Top of mast
Mate	1st 2nd and 3rd officers in chain of command
Meridian	True north/south line
Mizzen	Sail set on mizzen mast in fore and aft rig
Mizzen mast (1)	Aftermost mast in a ketch or yawl
Mizzen mast (2)	Mast 3rd from forward in vessel with 3 masts or more
Mizzen staysail	Fore and aft light weather sail set from mizzen mast
Monohull	Single hulled vessel
Mooring	Permanent Anchor with floating buoy for vessel to pick up
Mouse	To make turns round a hook with yarn to prevent unhooking
Naval Pipe	Deck fitting through which anchor chain passes
Neap Tide	Small tides between full and new moons
Nip	Sharp bend in a rope where it passes over a sheave or fitting
Oakum	Material made of rope yarns for caulking i.e. fill hull seams
On the Wind	See close hauled
Outhaul	Line to haul a sail into position along a spar
Overhang	Extended part of a vessel at bow or stern
Painter	Rope to secure dinghy or small boat when not in use
Palm	Sailmaker's tool to thrust needles through sailcloth
Parcel	To cover a rope, wire or splice with canvas prior to serving
Parrel Balls	Wooden balls strung on a line to hold a gaff or sail to mast
Partners	Framework supporting the mast at the deck
Patent Sheave	Block sheave with roller bearings
Pawl	Metal stop on a winch or windlass to hold the drum
Pay, to	To fill a seam or slack away a line
Peak	Uppermost corner of a gaff sail
Pennant	Pointed flag, also line used for reefing a sail
Pinrail	Wooden rack to hold belaying pins
Pintle	Rudder fitting to take gudgeons

Poop	Raised after deck in a vessel
Port	Left hand side of vessel when facing forward
Porthole	Circular window in ship's side also scuttle
Port Tack	When wind is on port side of vessel close hauled
Pram	Dinghy with square transom at both bow and stern
Preventer	Running or adjustable backstay
Puffer	Small coastal vessel unique to West of Scotland
Punt	Another name for dinghy or tender
Purchase	System of blocks and rope to increase power, see also tackle
Quarter	Midway between midships and aft
Raffee	Triangular sail set above uppermost yard on square rig
Rake	Angle of mast to deck in fore and aft direction
Ratlines	Ropes or battens secured to shrouds to facilitate climbing
Reach	Wind on vessel's beam
Reef	To reduce sail by tying or rolling up part of it
Reef Points	Short lines fixed to a sail to tie up loose sail when reefed
Reeve	To pass a line through a block or hole
Rhumb Line	The shortest distance between two points on a chart
R.I.B.	Rigid inflatable boat
Riding Light	White light shown at night to indicate vessel is at anchor
Rig	The whole arrangement of masts, spars and rigging
Rigging Screw	See bottle screw
Roach	Convex curve on edge of a sail
Rowlock	Fitting to hold oar in place whilst rowing
Royal	Square sail set above topgallants
Rudder	Flat hinged blade fixed at stern to direct the vessel's course
Run	To sail directly before the wind
Runner	Running or adjustable backstay, also preventer
Samson Post	Strong post at bow for mooring purposes
Scantlings	Dimensions of materials used for shipbuilding
Schooner	Fore and aft vessel with two or more masts
Scuppers	Holes on bulwarks to allow water to run off the deck
Sea	Nautical term for wave
Sea Anchor	Canvas drag to reduce vessel's speed in heavy weather
Seacock	Valve for through hull fittings
Seam	Joint between hull planks, also sewn seam on sail
Seizing	Binding together of two ropes or wires
Serve	To bind tightly with marline or twine
Set Flying	To set a sail with luff unsecured to a mast or stay

Set Up	To tension rigging
Sextant	Instrument used for astronomical navigation
Shackle	Metal fitting for joining chain, ropes or wire
Shake Out	To let out a reef
Sheave	Grooved wheel inside a block
Sheer	Curve of the deck line of a hull
Sheet	Rope to control clew of sail
Ship	Vessel of three or more masts square rigged on all
Shoal	Shallow
Shroud	Wire to support mast at side of ship
Skysail	Square sail set above royal
Slack Water	When tidal stream is stationary
Slip	Sloping hard surface for hauling vessel out of the water
Sloop	Single masted fore and aft rigged vessel with one headsail
Snap Shackle	Shackle fitted with quick release device
Snatch Block	Block with side opening to facilitate insertion of rope
Sole	Cabin floor
Soldier's Wind	Wind on the beam
Sound	To measure depth of water
Spanker	Fore and aft sail on aftermost mast in square rig
Spider Band	Metal band with belaying pins fixed to mast
Spinnaker	Light balloon type sail, for downwind work
Splice	To join ropes or wire or form eye by intertwining strands
Spline	Thin wooden strips inserted in hull seams
Spreader	Struts fitted on mast to spread stays (see also crosstrees)
Spring	Rope for mooring vessel to prevent fore and aft movement
Spring Tide	Maximum range of tide, opposite of neap tides
Spritsail	Four sided sail with spar from tack to peak
Square Rig	Sail set on horizontal yard swung across the vessel
Stanchion	Supporting column or pillar
Starboard	Right hand side of vessel when facing forward
Starboard Tack	When wind is on starboard side of vessel close hauled
Stay	Wire mast support
Staysail	Triangular fore and aft sail set on a stay
Steerage Way	When vessel has enough forward motion to enable steering
Stem	Foremost part of vessel to which planks are fastened
Stern	Aftermost part of vessel to which planks are fastened
Stiff	Vessel which stands up well to hard winds

Stopper	Temporary rope to hold lines under load
Stringer	Longitudinal timber strengthening member inside hull
Strum Box	Bilge pump strainer
Swell	Long seas (waves) that do not break
Tabernacle	Fitting enabling deck stepped lowering mast to be lowered
Tabling	Strengthening seam on edges of sail
Tack	Bottom forward corner of sail, or top corner of square sail
Tack, to	To work to windward in a zig zag manner
Tackle	System of blocks and rope to increase power, see purchase
Tafrail	Rail round stern of vessel
Take Up	Hull seams take up when they swell by immersion in water
Taut	Stretched tight
Teak	High density hardwood used in boat and ship building
Tender	Small open boat, see also dinghy
Throat	Upper forward corner of gaff sail
Thwart	Seats in an open boat
Tiller	Wood or metal bar attached to rudder for steering
Tingle	A copper patch to cover holes on a wooden hull
T.M.	Thames tonnage measurement for yachts
Top	Platform on top of each mast section in square rig
Topgallant	Square sail set above topsail on topgallant mast
Topgallant mast	Third mast section above deck in square rigger
Topmast	Second mast section above deck in square rigger
Topsail	Sail set on topmast
Topsides	Side of a vessel above the waterline
Topping Lift	Line to support the weight of a boom or yard
Transducer	Underwater fitting for echo sounder or log
Transom	Square shaped stern
Traveller	Ring fitting which travels along a spar to set sail
Treenail	Wooden fastenings used in traditional boatbuilding
Triatic Stay	Wire stays connecting schooner's foremast to mainmast
Trim	To sheet a sail to best advantage
Trimaran	A three hulled vessel
Truck	Circular wooden cap on top of a mast
Trysail	Small heavy sail used in place of mainsail in strong winds
Tumble Home	Convex curve of hull above the waterline

Underway	Moving through the water
Up Helm	Putting the helm to windward to change course
Vang	Rope or wire to control the end of a spar
Variation	Difference between true and magnetic north
Veer	When wind moves in a clockwise direction
V.H.F.	Very High Frequency, radio for marine communication
Wake	Disturbed water left by movement of vessel
Warp	Rope for securing vessel to dock or anchor, see hawser
Watches	Allocation of time for crew duty
Waterline	Where the ship's hull meets the water
Wear	To turn a vessel from one tack to the other by gybing
Weather	Windward side
Weatherly	Ability to sail close to the wind
Weather Shore	Land to windward of a vessel
Weather Side	Windward side of a ship
Weigh	To raise the anchor from the bottom
Winch	Mechanical device to tension ropes
Windlass	Mechanical device to raise anchor cable
Yankee	High cut jib used in cutter rig
Yard	Horizontal spar from which square sails are set
Yardarm	Outboard end of yard
Yawl	Two mast fore and aft vessel with mizzen aft of sternpost
Zulu	Scottish east coast sailing fishing boat

Appendix 6 – Useful Websites

British Waterways Board	www.britishwaterways.co.uk
Classic Boat	www.classicboat.co.uk
Classic Marine	www.classicmarine.co.uk
Clyde Cruising Club	www.clyde.org
Clyde Model Yachtyard	www.modelyacht.co.uk
Clyde Yacht Clubs Association	www.cyca-online.org.uk
Fairlie Restorations	www.fairlierestorations.com
Fife Regatta	www.fiferegatta.com
McGruer & Co	www.mcgruer-boats.co.uk
Old Gaffers Association	www.oldgaffersassociation.org
Royal Northern & Clyde Yacht Club	www.rncyc.com
Sail Training Association	www.tallships.org
Sail Training Ship - Christian Radich	www.radich.no
Scottish Maritime Museum	www.scottishmaritimemuseum.org
Tall Ship Friends	www.tallship-friends.de
The Eye of the Wind	www.eyeofthewind.net

Traditional Boats and Tall Ships   www.tallship.co.uk

Visit Scotland   www.visitscotland.com

Wooden Ships   www.woodenships.co.uk